CHIROLOGY

5 Realm

Counseling & Coaching

The Hand Reader's Guide

Jennifer Hirsch

Muse Press
P.O. Box 4892
Johannesburg 2128

Art design and typesetting by L J D

Cover design and photo of the author by Ken Etberg

A catalogue record for this book is available from the
South African Library.

Dedicated to the divine intelligence of the elemental kingdom and my teachers, clients and students, without whom I'd be void.

Contents

Introduction

When the first inspiration for the content of this book arose in me, I had no idea of what an intensely personal process the writing would become. This is largely because much of my life story is reflected in the words, but is just as as largely due to a core vulnerability and self-doubt that has plagued me from the get-go of my hand reading career; that of "here I am stepping deeply into the unknown dimensions of a stranger's psyche, and I am not officially qualified to do so."

In my early years of doing this work, there were few of the resources that today are available for 'lay' counselors and coaches to study coaching and counselling and coaching modalities. Thankfully, with the advent of life coaching as well as many other healing systems that offer to endorse students with enough proficiency to set up a therapy based practice, I have since studied several modalities and, in theory, my self-doubts are redundant.

Nevertheless, a residual lingers; to this day, even after plus 30 years of counseling people, the challenges I've had with assuming my own authority, with how to meet professional criteria and how to sustain a standard of competence still weaves their way through each of my days and even spills over into how qualified or not I feel about presenting these pages that so dabble in deep waters.

It's not just me. Many of my students over the years, as well as potential and practicing readers of all non-endorsed therapies struggle with the fact that their modalities aren't accredited as health services and that there is no global governing body that defines a measurable standard.

In the courses I teach, this question of there being no "official" qualification or license or accreditation available from external sources and that we are in essence individually charged with the responsibility of ascribing confidence to ourselves from within is a key theme that I emphasize for my students, who study the theory of chirology with great curiosity and interest, but find themselves feeling hesitant to practice. This, in part, is a focus of this book. While we chirology students are certified by our teachers, it is up to us to find confidence and to set a bar of proficiency for our counseling and coaching services.

Chirology is a craft that is composed of part science and part art. I have two ways of breaking down chirology's component parts. The first, which I spoke about in a previous book, is that the craft comprises 3 primary parts; the system of interpretation, the significance of intuition and how in your readings to not overthink and instead to allow intuition to flow, and very importantly, the counseling and coaching component of the how-to of verbal delivery. But for this book, I've further dissected chirology so as to help simplify the outline components of the craft.

A chirology reading is an interactive experience for both reader and client that can be likened to creating a weaving. To illustrate how readers weave the reading, I've divided the book into 4 parts, our system, our connection, the life situations, experiences and themes that clients present with and our communication. Each section has a governing element.

The earth element stands for the core of the hand reading experience. This is the 'loom', which in this analogy represents the infrastructure of all earth governed, practical, fundamental and scientific components of chirology. Ethical criteria, along with nomenclature of the hand's physical shapes, formations and textures is studied at this level. The 5 element system of ascribing element characteristics and principles to the hand features is rooted in the 'loom', the how-to of using the element based counseling and coaching model known as the 5 Realms of human experience. The 5 Realm model is the key focus of this book.

Also in the framework of a strong loom is some knowledge of the historical origins of palmistry, the essential basic of being comfortable with the intimacy of touching people's hands, a steadfast commitment to the work, the printing of the palms with ink, and for the professional practitioner, the ever-important method of hand print record keeping. I've called this section "Earth - Loom - System."

The water element brings 'textures' to the weaving. From the language of the elements, we draw on water principles and characteristics; water symbolizes service, and the receptivity, empathy, tenderness, care and love that readers offer.

Water is the governor and regulator of emotions. In deepening into emotional intelligence, we sense into and learn the words which best describe emotional nuances. Feelings need friendliness and room to unfold; in holding relaxed presence, we assist clients to connect to what they are authentically feeling. We observe that we have feelings about our feelings; examples of this are how we can be angry or terrified of our fear, afraid of our anger, sad about our sadness, ashamed of our shame. This awareness broadens the range of what is most alive within ourselves and our clients.

Also within the textures of the craft lies the principle of forgiveness, both of yourself as a reader who at times errs, and of the client, whose ways of being in the world may jar or dismay. We sustain a flow of fascination and inspiration for our craft; these too are water governed principles that relate to the 'textures' of chirology. Supervision, required in professional psychology, is yet another water governed ingredient; readers are well-advised to reach out for support. It's in this part of the book that I've shared my understanding of basic counseling and coaching, rapport, supervision and referrals. Included here are thoughts about how to avoid trying to rescue people, about working with family constellations, about the role of touch and the matter of crying in consultations. I've called this section "Water - Texture - Connection."

3

In the analogy of the hand reading experience being like a weaving, fire stands for the 'color'. The fire of the craft lies in the love, passion, energy and enthusiasm that we bring to the work of endeavoring to illuminate, motivate and encourage the people whose hands we examine. We need heart for hand reading; the craft takes a special brand of courage, a fire principle, to warm-heartedly engage with and speak our truth with a vast variety of people from all walks of life. In the psyche of man, the reading of hands, more than with any other divinatory tool, is laden with both negative association and unrealistic expectation. I quite often meet people who when they hear of my profession recoil energetically; they avoid connecting and even hide their hands behind their backs. Or the opposite, they thrust their hands towards me with an expectation that I'll instantly start reading their hands and even foretell something of their future. For sensitive readers, being met with fears, doubts and suspicion or with expectations that feel like demands are discouraging and inhibiting. In this context, true courage is meeting with what shows up with a relaxed and open heart.

In this fire governed section are 88 counseling and coaching situations, experiences and themes that clients often present with, along with some ideas and concepts I've worked with over the years. Each is listed under its primary governing element. This is not an exhaustive list of possibilities of what people go through, but does reflect what I've encountered in my plus 30 years of practice. Specialization, where focused intention is given to specific areas of our study, is another fire-governed component of the craft. I've called this section "Fire - Color - Fuel. "

With our spoken words being "the tools of our trade and the medicine of our profession", it is our air governed vocabulary and style of transmission that 'designs' the reading. Air represents thought and communication; what is the quality of our listening, how do we weave our words, and do we speak about ourselves?

Observation, another key air governed component, is part of the visual perceptiveness we develop so as to notice each nuance of hands and their gestures. Air element principles of research, theory, analysis, objectivity, investigation and conceptualization are all well-woven into the design of craft.

Impartiality, along with the capacity for detached compassion, are air level expressions of emotion which also have important roles in presenting a well-crafted hand reading experience.

In this section, which I've called "Air - Design - Communication.", I've presented a list of tried and tested professional counseling and coaching techniques, along with discussions on honesty, transference, imposter syndrome and burnout. The chapter ends with a guide on how to offer readings and how to optimally draw readings to a close. I've concluded with a few suggestions for building a professional practice.

While there is no chapter that is specifically devoted to how aether weaves through the craft of chirology, aether is the most significant element. Aether is the 'thread' of the weaving, it is the subtle binding agent, the intangible psychic and intuitively perceptive chiromantic magic that so mysteriously integrates and unifies the chirology experience; in fact, aether principles and characteristics pervade all dimensions of hand reading. The essence of aether infuses those moments of both verbal and energetic transmissions where no thought is involved and delivery just flows, as if we readers are simply channels. Aether's relevance is discussed in the 1st and 3rd sections of this book.

The word chirology (from Greek – *kheri* – hand, *logos* – knowledge) means knowledge of the hands. Chirology is a dialogue therapy that includes touching of the hands, intuitive perception and energy transference, offered within a counselling and coaching context.
With chirology, we fast-track self-enquiry via identification and analysis of the forms and structures of hands. As readers, we become

see-ers. When we let go of effort, we remember and know. The less effort we make, the more intelligent we are. The more we relax, the more intelligent we become.

To be a reader, you don't have to be a specialist in everything but it does help to know a little about a broad range of situations. My hope is that the contents of these pages inform and encourage you to do this work of supporting others' healing and growth with confidence and with heart-felt generosity.

"You can start learning, but you never finish. it goes on and on and the experience becomes deeper and deeper, higher and higher. The subtle arts are not only a question of expertise; they are more a question of love. Learn the technique and then forget it. When you learn deeply, ninety percent of the work is done by love, ten percent by the technique." Osho.

Earth

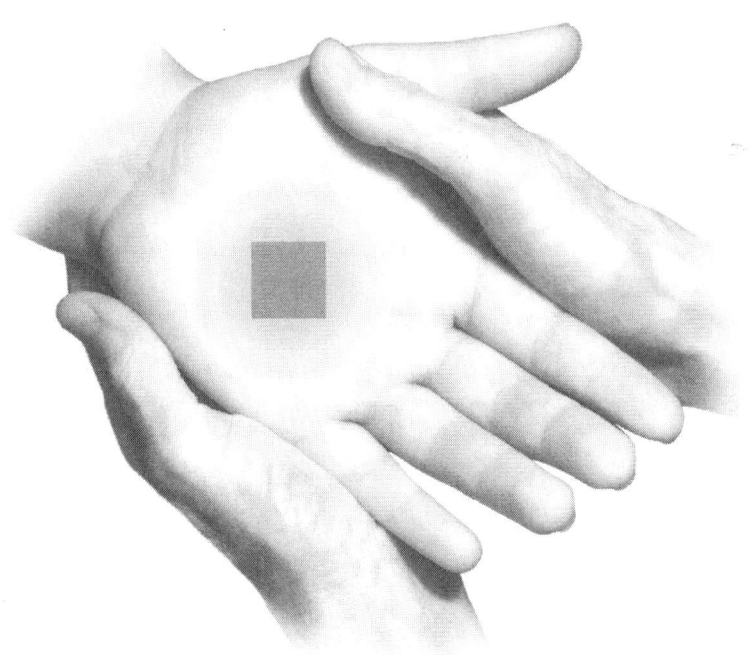

Loom ~ System

EARTH ~ LOOM ~ SYSTEM

The Language of the Elements

The elements earth, water, fire, air and aether provide a universal and dynamic language source for interpreting the forms and features of hands; the correlations of the elements to the realms of life and to each hand feature is fundamental to 5 element chirology's interpretive system. We define the unknown (the hands) in terms of the known (the element principles); individual variables of our hand's forms and markings and the areas of the hands on which the markings manifest are ascribed governing elements. Interpretation is structured around the associated element's principles and characteristics.

The substance of our existence is made up of various combinations of earth, water, fire air and aether. The inherent scientific principles of the elements, such as earth's solid reliability, water's flexible receptivity and sensitivity, fire's consuming energy and air's formless and spacious invisibility are naturally and intuitively known to us. From this, our innate foundation of comprehension and understanding of many behavioral characteristics of the natural elements, we easily learn more of their signature qualities and of how they interact with each other.

Since the process of offering readings is woven together with words, we look to the attributes and tendencies of earth, water, fire, air and aether to provide us with the concepts and vocabulary for the traits that are associated with each element governed hand feature. Features of the hands are like entry portals which open the conversation; through the correlations we enter the counselling and coaching themes.

The 5 Elements

In 5 element chirology, we use a symbol to represent each element: a square for earth, a circle for water, a triangle for fire, a cup for air and a teardrop for aether. The elements have individual governing contexts; these respectively are: I Matter, I Feel, I Act, I Think and I Am.

As energy vibrating at different frequencies, their manifestation is read upwards from the base. Slow, dense form is earth. The second higher frequency vibration is water, which can be touched, yet unless contained by earth has no form of its own. Vibrationally quick, restless, visible yet formless and untouchable fire is third in the tier. The pace quickens in pervasive, invisible air and culminates in transcendent, intangible aether. Symbolic of man's evolution from dull ignorance (earth) to spiritual consciousness (aether), we call this concept "The Principle of Graduated Materiality."

Using the associated colors of orange (earth), blue (water), red (fire), green (air) and purple (aether) is a helpful study aid for learning and remembering which element governs the various hand features.

Aether - I Am

Air - I Think

Fire - I Act

Water - I Feel

Earth - I Matter

- The Chinese/Taoist 5 element system describes earth, water, fire, wood and metal; in this system, the Greek/Western element air equates to the Chinese/Taoist element wood, and aether equates to the Chinese/Taoist metal.

Element Synergy

The compatible and opposing interplay between the elements in nature are reflected in the harmony or discord that we experience both subjectively and in relationships. Earth and water are yin, feminine, passive and downward directed elements, fire and air are yang, masculine, upward and active. Positive and negative traits, orientations and characteristics all find their resonance with one or more elements.

Conscious understanding of element traits helps us to better understand ourselves and others. The elements ceaselessly fluctuate within our physical, emotional and mental bodies. Health and harmony are present when they are balanced within, but for most, some will dominate, which causes others to be under-utilized. We instinctively seek to bring our elements into balance; even our being drawn to having direct contact with earth, water, fire and air in nature is self-regulating, balancing, remedial and healing.

Earth and water are complementary in that water nourishes earth, while earth contains, embraces and gives support to water. Swamps and mud characterize how water can weaken earth. Earth and fire are essentially incompatible; fire makes earth barren or damages through eruption, while earth puts out fire and creates soot and ash. Fire also relies on earth (matter) for survival, their marriage gives us the warmth of coal and embers. Earth and air oppose each other; earth is solid and air is intangible. Stuffy air and dust exemplify what happens when earth mixes with air, while sand and chalk are composed of air added to earth.

Water and fire are yin and yang antagonizing opposites. Fire distresses and evaporates water, while water inhibits fire and puts it out, but their qualities in combination gift us with hot water, saunas, steam and alcohol.

Fire and air are complementary elements; fire breathes and is activated by air (wind) and air is warmed by fire. Water and air are mostly incompatible. Air ruffles water, water clouds air, yet together these elements give us fragrances and bubbles.

The intricacies of the elements' exchanges with each other are represented in our hands. Through our personal element orientation, we understand the types of people we do or don't get along with. The hands of those with many fire and air features will get along well together. Those with many earth features in their hands offer pleasing security to water governed partners. An earth dominant person's stability will be compromised by too much fire; at the same time the fire type is bored with or smothered by earth traits. Air governed people need space, earthy routines or watery emotions restrict. Water archetype people are distressed by fiery intensity, while the water governed person dampens the latter's enthusiasm.

To ascertain the environment we feel most at home in, these same principles of harmonious vs discordant elements can be applied to the various combinations of hand shapes with skin textures.

Archetypes

The term archetype describes a collectively inherited unconscious idea, pattern of thought, image, or model that typifies particular people or things. There are hundreds of universal archetypes that, like everything else in existence, resonate with distinct elements, but in chirology we establish a foundation of four primary element archetypes.

Each unique personality profile is based on one of four hand shapes; earth, water, fire and air. While we are all combinations of archetypes, our archetypal hand shape represents the element that most flavors our character. In establishing their hand shape, we straight away understand some of that person's fundamental values, orientations and patterns of behavior. We are composed of combinations of elements but our hand shape category defines whether in traits and temperament, earth, water, fire or air predominate.

In chirology, our basic hand shape reveals the element through which we habitually express; shape shows our 'element of expression'. This assessment is the basis of a chirology analysis. The correlation of hand shape categories with their associated characteristics and traits is fundamental to all hand reading systems.

Our most dense element governs the areas of life that provide security. Nurturing earth is feminine; that which is buried is received, secured and contained, held in her womb. When we sit or lie on her we can sense her slow, steady and peaceful pulse. We feel her quiet receptivity and her comforting supportiveness.

Earth represents physicality; balance of earth in the psyche is evidenced in stable, down to earth types who have their feet on the ground. We see deficit of earth in frazzled, spaced out types; fire with its partner air have consumed earth. Overload of earth in a psyche shows up as inertia and complacency, suppressed emotions, procrastination and intractable opinions. People who are skeptical or prejudiced about self-inquiry or any kind of emotional or psychological excavation are constrained by earth.

When counseling and coaching with the 5 Realm model, we inquire: has the person's earth element swallowed, stifled and suppressed? Or is it fertilizing, soothing, strengthening and sustaining?

The Earth Archetype

In their physical realm, family, home and identification with community and country are central to the earth archetype person's value system. Earth people are by nature kind, supportive, protective and loyal, especially to family. Tradition is valued; they like old things, the good old days, and that which has stood the test of time. Regular mealtimes with the family and material security bring peace to earth types. Affinity with nature is likely. Wealth is built slowly and consistently. They are robust in physique and constitution and are seldom ill but may be predisposed to skeletal and digestive disorders.

In their emotional water realm, the practical earth type has the ability to be. They feel very deeply, yet are relatively easy-going, reassuringly agreeable and uncomplicated; they accept things as they are. Outwardly, they exude even-tempered and relaxed calmness and seem tolerant, unstressed and un-neurotic. Earth in nature is the only element that does not move unless it is moved; even when de-stabilizing upheavals occur in their lives, those with many earth governed features in their hands tend to avoid digging around in feelings. Self-analysis is not a natural default. Deeper emotions are likely buried, hidden even from themselves. What hurts them is violation of trust; they have an innate sense of honour, integrity, loyalty and honesty, and are profoundly affected by injustice. Sexually, the earth archetype person has a sensual and reliably steady desire nature.

In their vocational fire realm, earth types are cautious, change resistant and risk averse. Preference is for sticking to a long-lasting and repetitive job where they can maintain a systematic and structured routine. Reliability, patience and conscientious are characterized, responsibilities are taken seriously. The archetypal earth person dislikes the rat race. We find earth archetype people in professions that help others to feel supported and secured, such as home making, civil service, hospitality and anything to do with provision of food. Earth types are often good with their hands and make capable builders, farmers, craftsmen and mechanics.

In their mental air realm, they are calmly grounded. For the level-headed earth type, the moment is enough unto itself. Their intellectual orientation is cautious, sceptical, stubborn and fixed in opinion, with scant measures of imagination and originality of thought. Many earth people have an aversion to technology. Slow in absorbing and assimilate new ideas, pragmatic earth types are suspicious of the new and will endeavour to maintain as much continuity as possible.

In the spiritual aether realm, earth archetype people adhere to the traditional belief systems followed by their father and his father before. These unpretentious and innately humble types have intuitive wisdom and understanding of life's most important values.

Earth Principles
I matter, stability, reliability, support, density, solidity, tangibility, firmness, security, heaviness, structure, order, endurance, continuity, conservation, preservation, repetition, stillness, quietness, strength, containment, fertility, conformism, tradition, routine, method, simplicity, dutifulness, slowness, sobriety, immutability.

WATER

Feminine, yin water is passive receptive in nature. With no shape of her own, she adapts to mould herself to fit a vessel or to flow around and seep into the earthy forms she encounters. She gives way and accommodatingly yields to her environment. Paradoxically, while water is our most sensitive element, she is also nature's strongest element. More powerful than earth and fire, water is the universal solvent that destroys just about anything in time; as much as water nourishes, she can be corrosive. Water wants more of itself; the river flows to merge with the ocean and when given a slope, a droplet of water will run like a rivulet to cohere with the next droplet it encounters.

Water represents emotions; balance of water in the psyche shows up in the emotionally intelligent person. When instead of working at solving problems we let go and allow for the alchemy of existence to dissolve them, we are in flow with our water element. Also, the water element within is the source for inspiration. People who dream, who let themselves be carried away in their imaginations and then, by way of self-regulating, express through creativity, are in water element harmony. Deficiency of water is clearly evidenced in those with empathy deficit disorders. Weak water also shows in the inability to relax and to socialize. With excess water the person may imagine too much and see or believe in dark forces.

Other symptoms of water overload in the psyche show up as entrenched melancholy, depression and grief. Disillusion, despair and despondency pervade. The person is needy; they take everything personally and are draining to be with.

When counseling and coaching within the 5 Realm model, we inquire: is the person in flow? Are they drawing from the wellspring of potential adaptability and perseverance of their water element? Or are they insecure, sinking in muddy waters and absorbed in self-pitied introversion?

The Water Archetype

In their physical realm, water archetype people are the least constitutionally robust of the element types. They might be susceptible to allergies, water retention and bladder weakness and also to hypochondria. Material value is placed on that which beautifies, items of high quality and on elegance and style.

In their emotional water realm, subjective and sensitive water types are dismayed by the suffering of others and may self-sacrifice to assist. The question "How are you feeling?" is an expression of the water element. It doesn't take much to disturb them, they are hyper-responsive to their environments and easily upset. Moodiness, self-absorption and melancholy are characterized. Water type people are often susceptible to influence and manipulation. Romance might be more meaningful than physical and sexual intimacy. Most water dominant people seek to relate personally; companionship and close involvement with others, a secured emotional platform with the sense of safety when sharing feelings are highly valued.

In their vocational fire realm, cohesion, one of water's most significant principles, describes the water type's career orientation. Water features in hands reveal the people-oriented contact maker, the tribe gatherer, the natural-born public relations manager or events coordinator. Suited careers include social media, events, charities, human resources, healing, social welfare, nursing or any group endeavor where others are uplifted, enlightened and relieved, and where they have the sense of belonging. With their innate desire for and response to the poetic, harmonious and beautiful combined with their flair and elegance, we find water governed people in beauty therapy, interiors, design, art, music and dance. Perseverance is a water principle; some water types are highly ambitious and are determined to get what they want.

In the mental air realm, subjectively introspective, visionary and idealistic water types are seekers who often dive into psychologically deep interior realms. Water archetype people are diplomatic communicators. Enough is seldom the moment unto itself, they have exacting standards for themselves and others, this trait may play out in academic ambitiousness.

In their aether realm, water people are often spiritual rather than religious. The esoteric, metaphysical non-material dimensions have allure; water types are fine-tuned to matters mystical and are often highly intuitive.

 Water Principles
I feel, sensitivity, emotion, cohesion, connection, passivity, receptivity, introversion, persistence, perseverance, malleability, adaptability, flexibility, permeation, intimacy, reflection, stillness, imagination, inspiration, love, empathy, illusion, the sinister, mystery, magic.

Unlike the elements of earth and water, fire is active, it has no form, nor can it be still; fire is our most intense and volatile element and is the greatest emitter of energy. All-consuming fire seeks outwardly and upwardly. Without voraciously consuming all it meets, it cannot survive. Transformational fire is the only element that turns everything it encounters into more of itself.

Fire represents doing; balance of fire in the psyche expresses in harmonious measures of evolving creative expression, in knowing when to rest and in capacity for kindness to self and others. Excessively rampant fire is exemplified in many of our creative greats who, in their craving for extreme experience, master-mind their own undoing; they effectively extinguish themselves through a frenzy of self-destructive over-consumption. With deficiency of fire, we typically observe inability to make pro-active decisions, apathy, lethargy, indifference and lack of any vitality or enthusiasm in people, as if they have a meagre capacity for living.

When counseling and coaching within the 5 Realm model, we inquire: is the person's internal fire out of control? Has their fire gone rampant and in what sort of ways? How do they create, and how do they sabotage? Or is their aliveness within dimmed, dulled, diminished and defeated to a state of near paralysis or impotence? Where is their will, their determination, and how willing are they to change?

The Fire Archetype

In their physical realm, fire types express energetic joie de vivre. Just as fire shoots its flames assertively heavenwards, the true fire person reaches for peaks of experiences and lives life to the max. Fire types have vigorous metabolisms and robust constitutions but because of their impulse to 'burn the candle at both ends' are prone to stress related ailments such as high blood pressure. Inflammatory conditions are also characterized, but fire types burn off viruses and fight diseases more aggressively than any of the other element archetypes.

In their emotional water realm, fire types are pragmatic realists who can be impatient and intolerant of more subjectively emotional types. Rather than bearing grudges, they aim for the future and prefer to be done with the past. In long-term relationships, peaceful could equal boring; conflicts and melodramas might infuse. Sexually, the archetypal fire person desires intensity, excitement and passion.

In their vocational fire realm, enterprising, decisive and ambitious fire types are the achievers. Fire types are restless, impatient and have a low boredom threshold which motivates for an enthusiastic interface with life's promise. Routine work which leaves no room for spontaneity sets tiresome limits on the always busy fire type's innate get up and go, but this experiential orientation can tip them towards workaholism and burn-out. These are the goal-orientated, ego-centered leaders, strategic entrepreneurs, project managers and creative artists; people who effect change and progression. Fire-driven people are in their element in publically visible, influential careers such as politics, the military, corporate management, sport, film and trading.

In the mental air realm, strategy and intensity of focus that tips towards obsession characterize the orientation of the fire archetype person's thinking. The urge in impulsive fire is towards freedom; fire types desire and purposefully seek the new. For these often astute and strategic thinkers, the time it takes for thought to become deed and for actions to show results might be a trial of patience.

In the spiritual aether realm, it's in the evangelistic religious leader that fire is clearly expressed. Fire is also alive in our influential life coaches who passionately campaign for enlightened living.

Fire Principles

I act, doing, energy, intensity, action, change, transformation, risk, purification, courage, ferocity, creativity, warmth, focus, initiative, enthusiasm, quickness, illumination, will, vitality, spontaneity, extroversion, creativity, strategy, direction, leadership, inflammation, radiation, ego, hate, anger, cruelty, destruction.

Formless, shapeless and invisible air cannot be tangibly touched, has no substance and is the most refined of the elements. Ineffable and weightless moving air affects the world around us, we feel how it flows as we breathe, we sense it lightly touching our skin and hair, yet we cannot easily see or describe air.

Air represents the intellect; balanced air is exhibited in the self-reliant, discerning and insightful thinker, the person who seeks furtherance and who has both wisdom and wit. Excess air in the psyche exhibits as emotional detachment, sometimes to the point of solitary isolation. The archetype of the intimacy-avoidant sexually unconventional voyeur applies here. Airy fairy people who are disassociated from their bodies, who barely know their own feelings and minds, who are disturbed with thoughts about others' opinions are lost in the spaciousness of ungrounded air. Surplus air also shows up in nervous system overdrive, in our feeling wired, stressed and anxious. Weak air is indicated in those who are in a rut, where mental goals are stagnant and where there are no interests or capacity for discrimination or self-inquiry.

When counseling and coaching with the 5 Realm model, we inquire: is the person's air element like a dispersive hurricane that is blowing them and everything around them apart? Do they dwell in a private realm of coldness, criticism and contempt? Or does air express itself in the person's psyche as curiosity, as lively, communicative interest and as a light, free and up-lifting vibration?

The Air Archetype

In their physical realm, air types may suffer nervous system overdrive, anxiety, worry, insomnia and respiratory ailments; the air element governs our nervous and respiratory systems. Air types live in their heads; they tend to forget to eat. Money might be spent on novelty items.

In their emotional water realm, feelings are typically thought about, intellectualized, rationalized and impersonalized. That air is closest to space reflects in the air person's non-committal orientation; air types need freedom and independence. Sexual orientation can be curious, open-minded, unconventional and visual; optimally their partners are also their friends. In the air archetype we have a spectrum; some are private, introverted and solitary, while others are expansively extroverted.

In their vocational, fire realm, the archetypal absent-minded professor who absorbs in research to the exclusion of all else well-describes the air profile. Or, they become most animated in lively discussion, when communicating their ideas and understandings with others of like mind. Career orientation is towards philosophy, media, journalism, medicine, academia and writing; most curious, observant, investigative and inventive air people need variety. Other air resonant careers are astrology, astronomy, psychology, science, teaching, chirology, consulting, engineering, homeopathy and law.

In their mental realm, the air archetype person has an alert and penetrative mind. Thoughtful, curious and broadminded air types theorize, analyse, investigate and study. They dwell in the realm of the intellect, seeking to understand, to acquire knowledge and information and, with minimum prejudice or misinformation, to permeate to the essence of any matter. Distance, an air principle, helps us to understand that the air person observes their world objectively, while seeking an unbiased and impartial perspective.

The unfocused air person becomes distracted, dispersed and spread too thin, but the more balanced air type has a retentive memory and is a well-informed, informative communicator.

In the spiritual aether realm, air archetype people are motivated by the quest for understanding. Rather than aligning with any dogma or creed, air types are inclined toward deeper meanings; they gravitate to an applied philosophy rather than to any prescribed religion or watery spiritual belief.

 Air Principles

I think, analysis, theory, ideology, perspective, intangibility, formlessness, pervasion, dispersiveness, distance, expansion, individualism, innovation, freedom, perception, curiosity, information, knowledge, versatility, communication, eloquence, thinking, observing, analysing, understanding, detachment, impracticality, eccentricity.

Aether is the classical fifth element. This is the realm of life force; the animating universal energy which so alchemically exerts to matter. The term 'aether' has its origins in ancient Greece and in medieval western philosophy, where it is described as an element which has a manifestation of its own.

In chirology, the aether element represents spirit, that which never dies. Aether is essence, the God principle, the origin and source of the four material elements earth, water, fire and air; in the same way that light refracts into colours, aether vibrates in the varied frequencies of the four tangible elements. Aether's innate principles integrate and unify earth, water, fire and air.

In the aether realm we honor and respect people's religious beliefs and spiritual orientations. Within the spectrum of the aether realm, clients might share of their faith and about the comfort they find in their religious and spiritual affiliations. For others, this sometimes denied and sometimes acknowledged realm can be deeply associated with disillusion and the pain of separation, of not having any connection to our Creator.

While all the world's religious persuasions fall under the umbrella of aether, the God principle, it's interesting to observe that every religious and spiritual persuasion has its own elemental resonance.

Styles of devotional practice clearly reflect an associated element; earth governs the old nature and tribal religions, such as paganism, shamanism, fertility cults and ancestor worship. Shinto, one of Japan's two main religions, and the traditional patriarchal religions of Judaism and Christianity, are also governed by earth. Earthy devotion is obedient, dogmatic, belief bound, duty oriented and is practiced with persistence and regularity.

Hinduism, with its God Brahman who takes on a myriad of forms that many Hindus worship as gods or goddesses in their own right, is the main water religion of the world. Spiritual orientations that are polytheistic, flexible, mystical, symbolic or linked to lunar worship are also categorized under the water element. Charismatic Christian worship is another example of how, like water in nature, people follow their urge to merge and to sing God's praises. Water expresses herself in styles of spiritual practice that are loving, forgiving, faithful, compassionate, service oriented, selfless, devoted to others' welfare and non-violent.

Fire rules any fundamentalist Christian, Islamic, Judaic or other religious belief in a God who is wrathful, vengeful and omnipotent. Fiery religious practice is organized, evangelistic, warlike (as in holy wars), vigorous and zealous. Emphasis is on doing of deeds in the name of the belief.

Buddhism is the air religion of the world. Perhaps more philosophical than religious, Buddhism teaches wisdom and realization. Any person of any other religion can take refuge in Buddhism. Air level spiritual practice is reflected in contemplation, meditation, mantra, study of scriptures and sacred books and the search for higher truth and understanding.

Aether also governs the mysterious non-material realm of intuitive perception that is inextricable from the hand reading craft. As readers, we tap into the aether frequencies of consciousness, compassion, energy transference and channeling.

When counseling and coaching within the 5 Realm model, we explore people's religious and spiritual formative influences and current time relationship with their spiritual resources.

 Aether Principles

I AM, enlightenment, consciousness, religion, spirituality, essence, divinity, sanctity, integration, wholeness, unification, channeling, peace, compassion, transcendence, karma

- Other concepts for aether are space, void, vacuum, quintessence, shunya and akasha.

- In previous writings, because of the first three letters of the word chirology, I used poetic license; I replaced the classical western fifth element concept of 'aether' with the Taoist concept 'chi'. Chi represents prana, dynamic vital energy, life force and the fundamental life principle. While chi is technically not defined as an element, the non-material concepts and principles of both aether and chi can be ascribed to the fifth (spiritual) realm.

The 5 Realms

The 5 Realm counseling and coaching model is core to chirology and is the hand reader's greatest asset and tool. The domain of each individual realm is governed by an element. In readings, delivery of information is interwoven with intuitive perception and channeling and is specifically offered within the context of the 5 Realms.

Aether – Spiritual

Air – Mental

Fire – Vocational

Water – Emotional

Earth - Physical

The 5 Realm Counseling and Coaching Model

The 5 Realms identify, define, holistically encompass and embrace the constituent parts of our multi-dimensionality; the construct represents wholeness (holiness). The realms classify into specific component parts or clusters of all areas of human experience.

When presented within the 5 Realm model, the hand reading experience is significantly optimized; consciously inviting in relevant counseling and coaching themes that are intrinsic to the 5 Realms both expands and integrates the essential quality of readings.

Spiritual
Pertains to the sphere of religious and spiritual life.

Mental
Describes intellect, psychology, dimensions of communication (subjective and with others), hobbies and education.

Vocational
Defines domains of life purpose and vocation, joie de vivre and fundamental available energy for living. This realm incorporates the measure of evolving creative expression verses inhibiting, self-sabotaging behaviors.

Emotional
Relates to well-being and functions of emotional balance, social conscience, friendships, familial relationships, intimacy and sexuality.

Physical Categorizes those aspects of life that provide security; health, family, home life, country and finances.

Using the 5 Realms as an Interactive Process

Readings are designed to identify and to bring to balance the inherent functions of our physical, emotional, vocational, intellectual and spiritual realms. Every person has longings for happiness in the various spheres. When we have excess in some areas, there are deficits and consequences in others, and when our 5 Realms are in balanced inter-relationship, we feel more harmoniously integrated.

Before or during readings, it can be helpful and interesting for clients to receive a concise explanation of how the language of the elements is used to interpret hands, how each hand feature is assigned an element rulership and that we define the unknown (the hands) in terms of the known (the principles of the elements).

This brief outline can then lead to our sharing with clients a basic definition of the 5 Realm model; that it is composed of the physical, emotional, vocational, mental and spiritual layers of experience; in this way we bring the component parts of their lives to their awareness, which in turn facilitates a greater sense of potential insight and integration into their consciousness.

In dialogue, each realm, even if briefly, is mentioned. Use a diagram, or list the facets of each of the realms on paper. Do a checklist of positives and deficits; this is a practical way to illustrate, pinpoint and articulately communicate the person's sources of struggles, their promise and potentials and their joys and successes.

Hands

Hands from a distance

Professional chirologists/chirologers (both terms are correct) observe the hands' shapes, textures and markings to identify people's emotional climates, sensitivities, needs, preferences and vocational aptitudes, but even for those of us who know nothing about chirology, a mere glance at a set of hands will often in a flash of intuitive perception reveal highly accurate information about that person. Unknowingly and without conscious awareness we calibrate each other's hands and intuitively sense a broad range of people's qualities, such as for example kindness, friendliness, laziness, or that they are hard-working.

As a reader, the most noticeable feature in a set of hands first commands our attention. This can be a good point of departure for the reading. I quite often begin with "The first thing I noticed about your hands is......" Every nuance of shape, form, marking and gesture informs. We attune to and gauge gestures, size of hands in relation to body size, what types and where rings are placed, what their handshake, hand consistency and moisture or dryness reveals, any shakiness and the textures and quantity of hair on the backs of hands. From a distance we can also observe the general lengths of fingers, the size and forms of thumbs, depths of lines, color in palms and nails, and general nail condition.

Gestures

First to catch the eye might be gesticulation. Broad-minded, open and friendly traits are likely in those with expressive and expansive hand gestures, especially if their fingers are held widely opened. When fingers are held close and movements are reserved or even hidden at sides or behind backs, owners are more private and guarded. Anxiety is evidenced in the holding of thumbs.

Size

Large hands show that the owner is thorough, patient and detail oriented. Responses are more considered than in the more impulsive small handed, who might be easily distracted, yet can see the bigger picture, make the best managers, have quick responses and are good in emergencies. Ignore this if the person's hand size fits their form.

Rings

Rings are chosen for their beauty, or because they fit, or as significators and symbols, such as in rings worn by men in political, religious or military roles, or to signal marriage. Most rings are worn without any conscious awareness of the significance of choosing a particular digit, the associated qualities of which might be deficient. Since rings add weight to the qualities of each finger, conscious placement can enhance the strengths associated with that finger. Wearing no rings is a positive indicator.

Handshake

Take into consideration that different cultures have associated styles of handshakes. For westerners, limp, soft handshakes show lack of energy and apathy, and possibly depression or illness. Firm shakes show practical energy and vitality. Bone-crushing shakes reveal insensitivity or even a cruel streak. A hand held longer than necessary wants something, or is seductively signaling attraction.

Consistency

Softness or hardness is assessed during a handshake but can also be observed from a distance; one can often see from gestures if hands look firm or notably supple. The softer the hands, the lesser the physical energy and the more the person can be manipulated. Yet soft handed people might be manipulative, astute and shrewd. Hard hands with no 'give' to the flesh show realism and energy. Emotions may be repressed. The hard handed are more skeptical and unyielding. Emotions may be repressed. The person is more skeptical and unyielding. They prefer getting on with life to 'emotional excavation'.

Tremoring

Some people suffer constant shakiness without any definable cause; the involuntary quivering of their hands is a fairly common and benign neurological condition known as the essential, familial or idiopathic tremor. Tremoring is also caused by stress, shock, caffeine, and is a side effect of alcohol, recreational drugs and medications. Consider too the gradual weakening of the nervous system due to aging and degenerative illnesses.

Hair

The thicker the hair on the backs of the hands, the earthier or fierier the person. No hair is a water feature, while sparse hair is air governed.

- For in-depth tutorials on reading the hands, please refer to the publication "Illustrated Chirology Palmistry and Hand Reading".

Right and Left Hands

We read both hands. The hand used to sign with is the active hand. Distinct differences in the features of set of hands add complexity to the person's interior climate; there is a disparity between what they show and what they keep private.

Active hands represent our persona, that is, our projected personality, the conscious mind and traits we have greater awareness of. In active hands, we read something of future potentials and patterns that are most likely to continue.

Passive hands reflect true character and temperament, subconscious psychological dispositions, formative influences, instinctive emotional responses, deeper desires, inherited, private or hidden traits, as well as potential talents. Temperament is how we think, react and behave. Character forms from conscience, and the moral orientations that influenced us in childhood.

A messily lined passive hand with an active hand that has clear, strong lines evidences a progressional trend; for this person, formative influences and past difficulties may have been consciously addressed. Someone with a messy and stressed active hand and a clearer, stronger appearing passive hand might be facing challenging obstacles.

Palm Prints

The gathering of people's hand prints is essential to the work of the professional chirologist. While we can read from the hands directly, a good quality print gives a clear map of the flows of energy of the lines and glyphs. Palm prints also serve as study references and for observing changes in lines when in future years the person's hands are re-printed.

The art of taking handprints is acquired with practice. Stroke the skin and observe the hand's forms textures and shapes. Look for any features that jump out and feel for any energy resonances that might exude. Dry, roughish skin texture will need more ink, whereas moist skin needs less.

Materials

- several layers of newspaper
- a smooth tile or piece of glass
- a hard roller - minimum 10cm is best
- ink - Rolfes Lino. Black is best
- A4 copy paper
- a table to work on

Technique

1. Position the wad of newspaper on a table with the edges just overlapping the edge.
2. Position your tile, roller, ink and copy paper on the newspaper.
3. Apply a little ink onto the tile and spread with the roller. The purpose of the tile is to distribute the ink so as to get it evenly onto the roller.

4. Take the person's one hand and with long strokes, roll ink evenly onto their palmar surface. Include finger and thumb tips.

5. Ask the person to place their hand lightly (no pressing down) and in its most natural position onto the paper. If the palm has no hollow, press down gently, then ask them to lift up their hand directly. If the palm is hollow (most people have some hollow), instruct them to hold the newspaper steady with their other hand. Keeping their hand level with the table, slide the hand and the paper off the edge, while gently pushing upwards into the hollow from under the newspaper.

6. Peel paper off.

7. Repeat with the other hand.

8. Write the name, date, date of birth, and whether they are right or left hand active. Make a note of scars, moles, warts, nail shapes, hair, flexibility etc. or anything else which might be relevant.

• If you don't have a print kit, try using a light layer of red lipstick.

• To practice training your eye, do outlines of your own and other's inked or non-inked hands (and thumbs separately) with a vertically held pencil.

• A good quality magnifying glass is an essential requirement.

Shapes of Hands

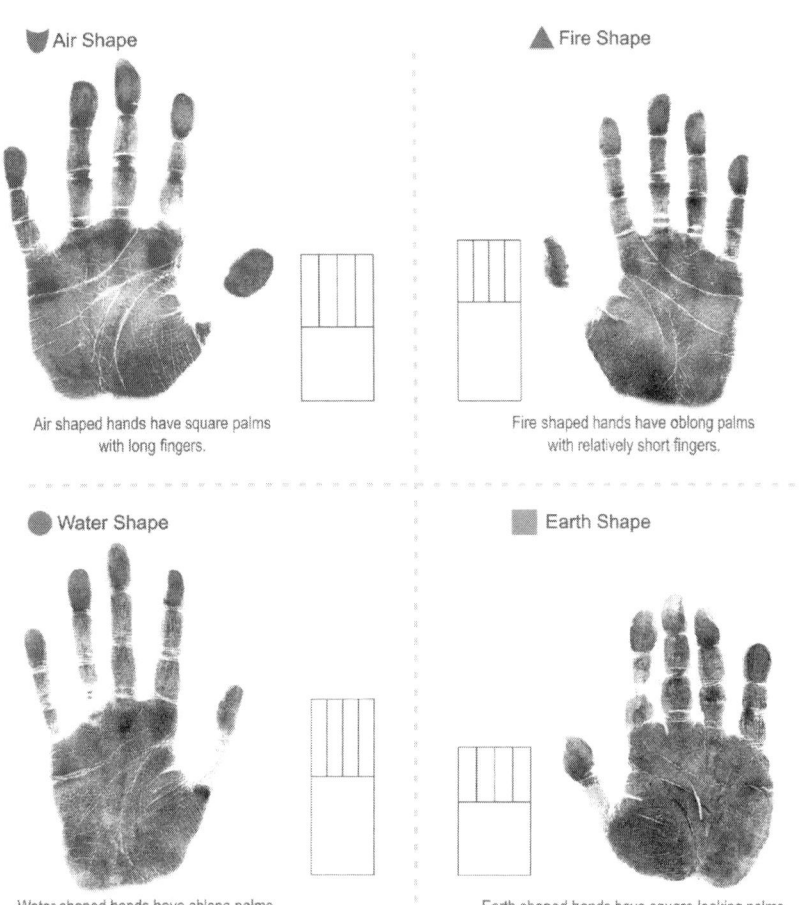

Air Shape

Air shaped hands have square palms with long fingers.

Fire Shape

Fire shaped hands have oblong palms with relatively short fingers.

Water Shape

Water shaped hands have oblong palms with long fingers.

Earth Shape

Earth shaped hands have square looking palms with fingers that are short in relation to the palms.

Hand Shape ~ Measuring

Shape is always measured from the palmar side. We compare the shape of the palm with the relative length of the fingers. Palms are evaluated as being either square or oblong, and in relation to palms, fingers are either short or long.

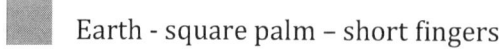 Earth - square palm – short fingers.

 Water - long palm - long fingers.

 Fire - long palm - short fingers.

 Air - square palm – long fingers.

1. On either the live hand or the palm print, measure the palm's length from the base where it joins the wrist, up to the base of the earth (middle) finger.
2. Measure the width of the palm, from just above where the thumb protrudes, across to the ulnar (baby finger) side.
3. Measure the length of the earth finger.

- If the width is almost (within a cm or so) as wide as the length, the palm is square.
- If the palm is narrower by 1.5cm or more, the palm is oblong.
- Fingers are almost never as long as palms, but when they measure within 1.5cm as long as the length of the palm, they are long.

Some people's hands defy exact classification; they have features of a second and sometimes a third shape. In this case, intuitive perception, in combination with examination of skin texture and dermatoglyphics, will inform the reader of the person's basic archetypal orientation.

Skin

Palmar skin texture is like a membrane through which we experience life. While hand shape represents how we express ourselves, the four skin textures represent our elements of impression; they signify styles of subjective responses the world makes upon us and reveal something of the environments we'd be happiest in. To decide skin texture, we lightly run our fingertips over the palms and fingers on the insides of the hands.

 ### Earth
Feels dry, very rough, leathery and warm; the skin ridges and pores are visible and clearly felt. Those with earth skin texture are practical, at home in the physical, material realm, have rapport with nature and are not given to emotional and mental analysis.

 ### Water
Feels moist, smooth, soft, fleshy, pale and warm; the skin ridges and pores can't be seen or felt. Those with water skin texture are feeling-centered, sensitive, intuitive and idealistic.

 ### Fire
Feels dry, roughish, firm, reddish, warm or hot; the skin ridges and pores can be seen. Those with fire skin texture are active, easily bored, forceful, quick, spontaneous and assertive.

 ### Air
Feels dry, smooth, pale and cool; the skin ridges can be slightly seen and felt. Those with air skin texture are observant, analytical, research oriented and communicative.

- Sometimes people's palms have more than one skin texture, for example, dry palms with moist fingertips; in which case interpretation is based on the blending of the characteristics of the differing elements.

- Moist fingertips might signify a temporary emotional crisis for example, a divorce process or recent shock.

- Users of tobacco, alcohol and other drugs and people who are in substance use withdrawal often have sweaty palms.

- Aether has no ascribed skin type.

- A translucent glow to the skin on the tops of the hands indicates activated aether principles; this is a sign of a spiritual and intuitive person.

- Hands that are always sweaty and moist suggest anxiety, nervousness and stress. Perspiring hands generally show heightened emotions. Person is vulnerable, perhaps insecure, dependent and unconfident. Their ideals are strong and they need co-operation, not conflict.

- Palmar hyperhidrosis is a medical disorder characterized by excessive sweating of the hands.

- Firm, dry handshakes signify confidence, while moist, damp or clammy handshakes generally indicate vulnerability, anxiety and stress.

Skin Color

The variations of color of the hands indicate certain emotional and personality traits. Colors also have health indications. Take the natural and cultural skin color into consideration.

Red

Person is energetic, ardent, enthusiastic and may have difficulty with moderation. Can also signal circulatory issues. Red Moon mounts suggest worry about or anger at someone they love.

Blue

A sign in hands of moodiness, poor circulation, depression, deep hurt and sadness.

Yellow

The person is predisposed to negativity and crankiness, they worry a lot and are self-critical.

White

Pale hands reveal self-centeredness, low energy and idealism but might also show ill-health. Vitality is low, the person needs alone time and can't handle too many demands being made on them.

Pink

A positive indicator of warmth and kindness, but if accompanied by white splotches, suppressed anger is likely.

Shape and Skin ~ Binary Analysis

The binary analysis of shape and skin is the basis for vocational guidance in chirology. Hand shapes describe the style of how each person 'gives', while skin textures define the environment to which we are best suited, in other words, how we 'take'; this assessment is key to determining the environment in which we feel most 'in our element'.

These interpretations can be developed by using the principles of each element and applying the characteristics and traits to element combinations. We relate the hand shape to the skin texture; are they elementally compatible?

A set of fire shaped hands accompanied by compatible air skin texture reveals their owner to be active (fire) and curious (air); with air, fire acquires momentum and energy.

Spontaneity is dampened by water skin texture in a set of fire shaped hands; here the owner needs empathy and emotional support. People with long, slender and moist watery hands wouldn't thrive in a fiery fast-paced corporate environment.

In a pair of earth shaped hands with moist skin, the water principle of perseverance can add tenacity to the earth person's already present steadiness of purpose.

Lines

Hands are receptors and emitters of countless impulses of sensory nerve signals from and to our brains, this brain directed activity registers as lines in our palms. The understanding that our palmar lines are a reflection of the aether element channelling through our psyches is fundamental to chirology. As with all of nature's designs, the interrelation between ourselves and our Creator reveals itself in our palmar patterns.

Each individual line is ascribed a governing element and associated areas of life; this gives the context within which to codify and interpret lines.

Lines are categorized into main, minor and subsidiary. Interpretation is based on their quantity, depth, length, flow, form and markings.

Main lines represent basic functions of life force, heart and brain, while minor lines reflect our autonomic nervous system and deeper internal activity.

- Lines in hands can change, sometimes quite significantly, especially if there has been a dramatic event in the person's life, or sometimes they change only very subtly over time.

- For an in-depth look at lines, please see the publication "Illustrated Chirology, Palmistry and Hand Reading."

Earth in Lines

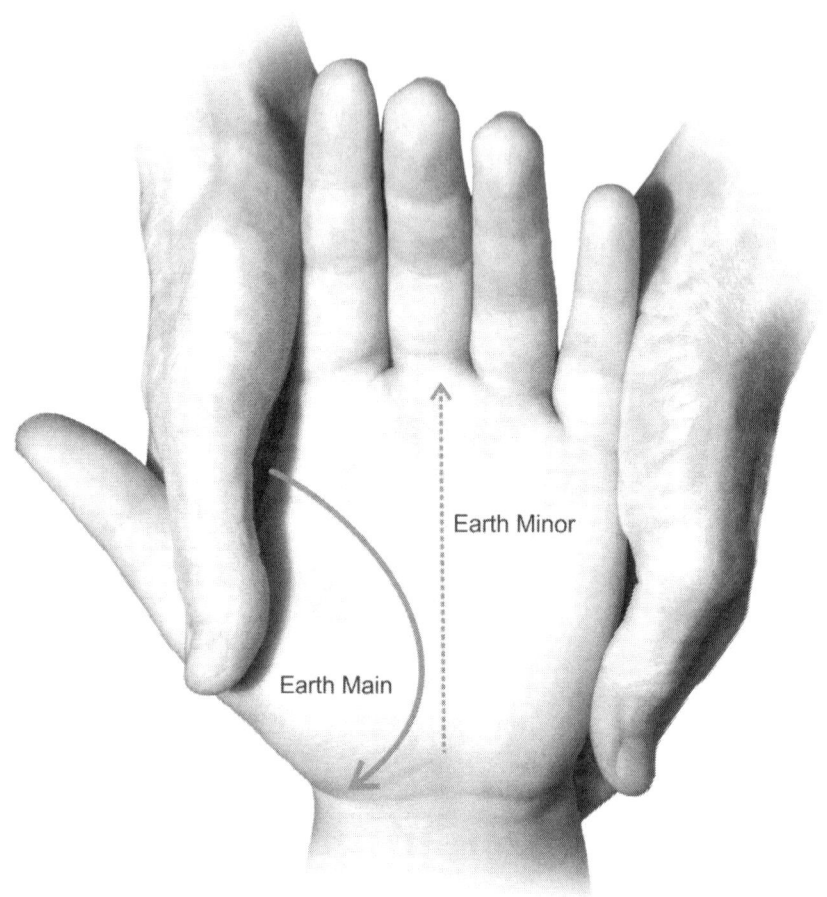

Earth Main

Earth (life) lines begin above the thumbs' protrusion and run down towards the wrists to encompass the balls of the thumbs. They represent the material realm, digestive and general health, vitality, attitude to money, the likelihood of moving or travel, and home and family life.

Earth Minor

Minor earth (fate/Saturn) lines begin from various possible starting points near the heel of the hand and run in the direction of earth fingers. They stand for internal balance, stability, responsibility, work ethic and life purpose.

Thick

Lines are rivers of energy; wide and shallow rivers flow more sluggishly than a narrow, deep river with a rapid strength to its flow. Thick lines suggest fatigue, lethargy and inactivity in the area of life that the line represents.

Few

Empty hands with few lines show a relatively calm, un-neurotic nervous system, uncomplicated psychology and a disinclination to self-analyze.

 ## Symbols and Markings - Earth Governed

Breaks - earth doesn't flow; the line ceases to flow - crisis, breakdown

Earth mount crease - horizontal line on Venus - integrity, loyalty, betrayal

Grilles - bar and activation lines collide - 'push/pull' conflicts

Squares - lines form a square - protection, teaching abilities

Water in Lines

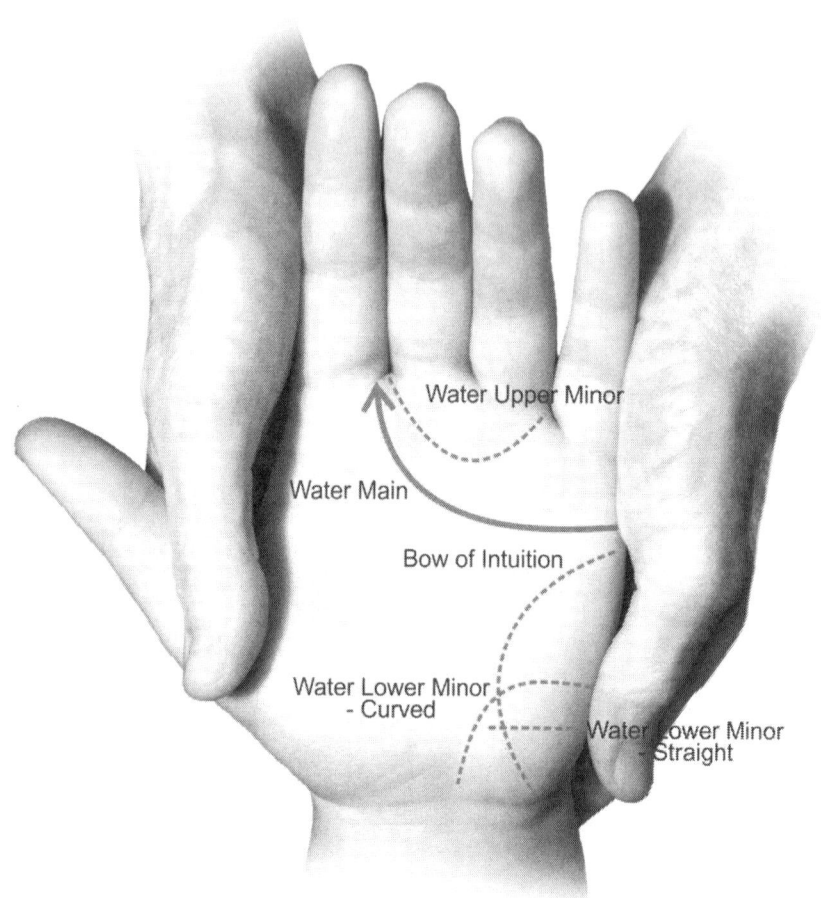

Water Main

Water (heart) lines begin on the ulnar side under air fingers and run across the palm to various end points. They represent how we relate to and connect with others and how we give and receive devotionally, emotionally and sexually. Water lines also point towards the health of the physical heart and chest.

Water Minor

Minor water lines have three differing manifestations, upper, lower in curved form and lower in straight form. Both the straight and curved forms might be present in one palm.

Water Upper Minor

The traditional 'Girdles of Venus' are curved, semi-circular lines which lie above water lines under earth and fire fingers. More accurately understood as being governed by the relatively recently discovered planet Neptune, they emphasize water orientations and represent emotional sensitivity, empathy, imagination, idealism, intuition, illusion, compassion and the spiritual quest.

Water Lower Minor - Curved

Curved lower minor water (allergy) lines lie over Moon mounts and often intersect earth lines near their base. They represent emotional and physical hyper-sensitivity and allergic responses to stimulus.

Water Lower Minor - Straight

The traditional 'via Lascivia'. These are transverse lines which cut across Moon mounts. They associate with obsession, jealousy, addiction and cravings for exhilaration and peak experience. More positively, their presence shows potential for focus, dedication and commitment. Although they are water governed, in the straight form they are strongly influenced by fire's intensity.

Bows of Intuition

Semi-circular arced lines which encapsulate Moon mounts are also called 'true lower minor water lines'; they relate to owners having precognitive hunches, a spiritual orientation and strong nurturing instincts.

Thin and Faint

Delicate lines reflect sensitivity, weakened life skills and low energy levels.

Wavy

Waviness in form and flow of lines add sensitivity and increased emotionality.

Symbols and Markings - Water Governed

Attachment lines - water lines run or send branches to start of earth lines - dependency

Chain - a series of islands - ongoing uncertainties

Children lines - cross, ascend or descend from relationship lines – children

Falling lines - downward falling flows - energy leaks, tiredness

Healing Stigmata - vertical lines under air fingers - healing, channelling

Islands - the line divides and weakens - loss of clarity, debilitation

Relationship (marriage) lines - horizontal lines on Mercury mount - quality of relationships

Rings of Solomon - lines on Jupiter mounts - innate wisdom, insight, empathy

Travel lines - horizontal lines on ulnar edge - restlessness, journeys

Fire in Lines

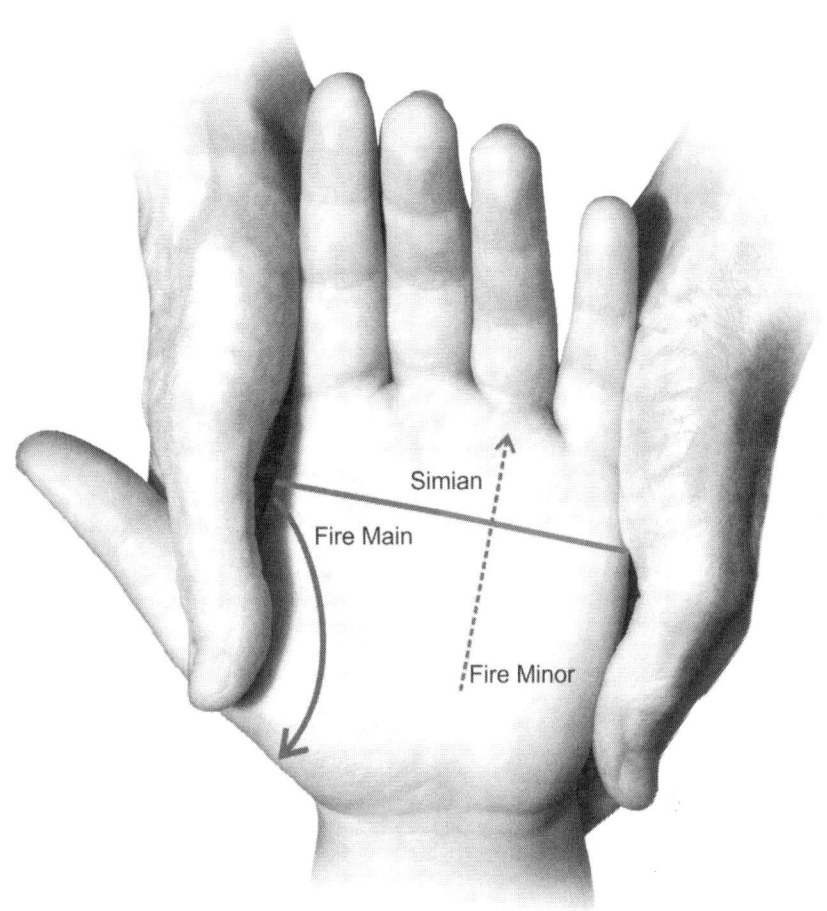

- Quadrangle - space between the water and air lines

Fire Main

Fire (Mars) lines run parallel to and inside earth lines on Venus mounts. They represent sources of strength. Physiology is strengthened when they originate directly from fiery Mars mounts, are deep and run parallel to earth lines, this adds enthusiasm and bravery. Many faint lines here show assistance from spiritual guides, angels and from supportive people.

Fire Minor

Minor fire (Apollo/Sun) lines begin from several possible starting points lower in the hands and run vertically over Sun mounts towards fire fingers. Minor fire lines reflect to an inner point of spiritual reference, luck, creativity, enthusiasm, optimism, public recognition and financial success.

Deep

Deeply etched lines reveal energy and vitality, with capacity for engaging in and coping with life. The added fire energies might aspect the owner experiencing many dramatic crises. Some traditional hand readers say that deep lines show the 'old soul'.

Straight

Any line that is well-defined, bold and straight is influenced by fire element qualities and characteristics, such as intensity and stamina.

Simian

Fused water (emotion) and air (thought) lines that form only one horizontal line across the palm are simian lines. The quadrangle* is entirely missing. Emotions and thoughts are intertwined. Simian lines add fire influence; inner intensity is experienced. Additionally, interpretation might be more water influenced when the lines float free and separated from the beginning of earth lines, and more air influenced when firmly joined to earth lines.

Symbols and Markings - Fire Governed

Activation lines - vertical lines on fingers - energy, stress

Ambition lines - upward branch from earth line - aspiration to betterment

Bars - small crossing or horizontal lines - blockages, obstacles, stress

Crosses - X like lines - opposition, fighting spirit, metaphysical interests

Dots - indentations in lines - inner stress, crisis

Pentagrams - service, spirituality, power

Rising lines - ascending branches - energy, efforts being made

Spikiness - like barbed wire - conflict, disruption

Stars - shock, crisis, conflict, illumination, psychic ability

Tridents (on mounts) - success, determination

Air in Lines

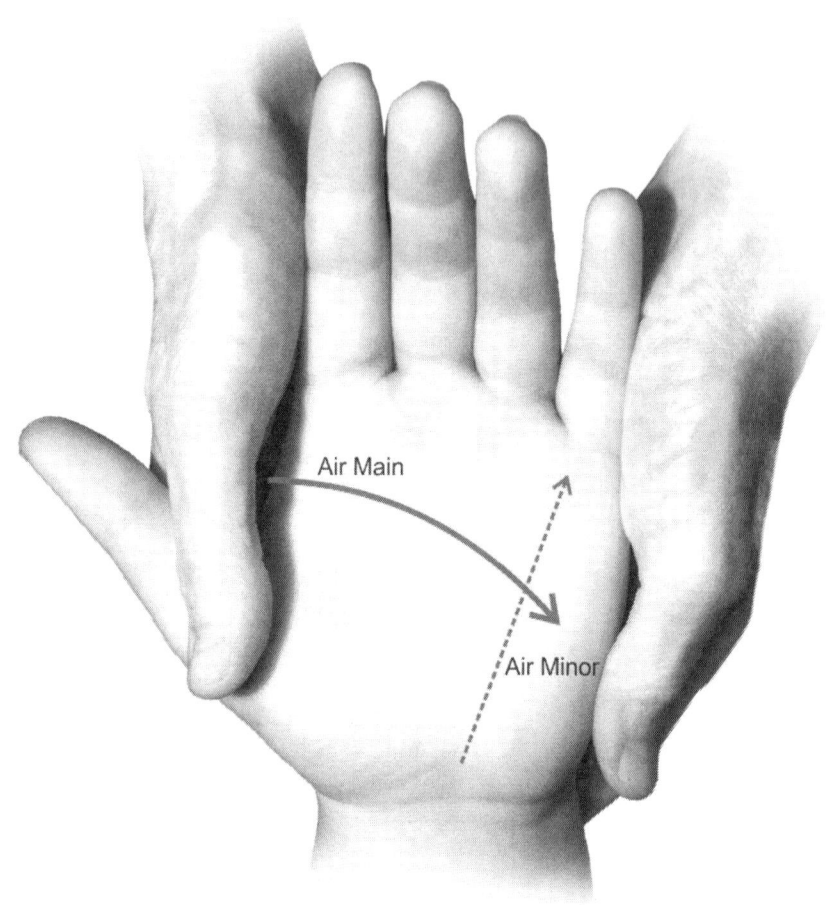

Air Main

Air (head) lines begin on the radial (thumb) side, either joined to, above or below the start of earth lines. They run in straight or curved forms transversely across palms. They represent the quality of our mental life, intellect, cognition, communication, interests, and how we receive, think about and transmit information.

Air Minor

Minor air (Mercury) lines mostly lie diagonally, between Mercury mounts under air fingers and the lower section of earth lines. Their presence suggests that the mind (air) is interfacing with bodily function (earth). They represent the autonomic nervous system, health (digestive and respiratory systems), intuition and business acumen.

Many

Full hands with a complex array of lines reveal over-active air; constant thinking, nervous system overdrive, worry, tension, anxiety and neurosis are characterized.

Clear - Curved

Clearly etched lines with graceful curves add air influence; qualities of communication and analytical curiosity are highlighted.

Symbols and Markings - Air Governed

Cramp lines - hover independently, they float freely below ends of main air lines - tension, intensity in mother relationship

Detachment lines - hover independently, they float freely above ends of main air lines - mental disassociation, detachment

Duplication - closely parallel lines - duplicity, two simultaneous situations

Fish - diamonds with 'tails' - seeking of furtherance, researcher

Forks - line ends in two or three prongs - versatility, acumen, judicial qualities

Furriness - cotton wool appearance to the line – anxiety

Joining lines in quadrangles that connect water and air lines - protocol, manners

Overlaps - line ends, another begins separately to run concurrently – change

Striations - dispersed lines, composed of bits and pieces - poor concentration

Tassels - line disperses into frayed ending - dissipation, poor resources

Triangles - mental acuity, aptitudes

Triplication - triplicated parallel lines - divided loyalties, protection

Dermatoglyphics

Glyphs [from dermatoglyphic - derma (skin) – glyph (writing)] are the skin's papillary ridge patterns that cover the entire inner surface of our hands. Glyph patterns are formed in the womb and never change through the course of a lifetime. Aether governed glyphs are patterns of cosmic energy that reflect our unique design. Not only do they mark our identity; they are understood to be energy portals or thresholds through which to perceive temperament characteristics and traits.

Glyphs are composed of four primary patterns: arches, loops, triradii* and whorls. Together these four earth, water, fire and air governed shapes form four primary classifications: arch, loop, tented arch and whorl, plus two additional composites, or combinations of patterns, the double loop and the peacock's eyes. A seventh category called 'accidentals' or 'variants' describe the occasional indistinguishable dermatoglyphic pattern.

- Triradii ('tri' – three and 'radius' – ray, or spoke - singular - triradius) occur when dermal ridges that flow from three different directions converge.

Earth in Dermatoglyphics

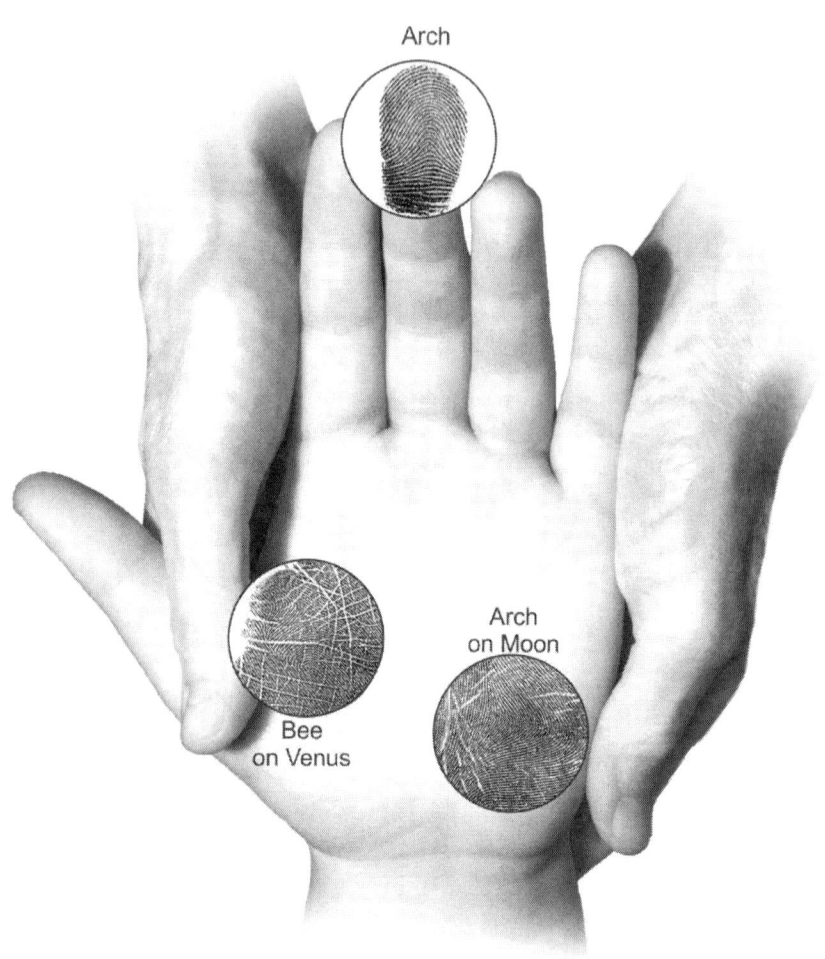

Arch - digital

The arch flows across the fingertip from one side to the other; it has no triradius. Arches look like simple hills that exude solidity and steadiness. Owners have dependable, kind and serious-minded traits.

Arch on Moon - palmar

A simple arch rests on a Moon mount, effectively stabilizing the Moon's emotional realm. Inner calmness, constructive imagination and practicality are characterized.

Bee on Venus - palmar

An anomalous, elliptical shaped, irregular patch of skin ridges on the upper mount Venus that flow against the grain of the surrounding ridges. Bees aspect an emotional response in their owner to all types of music.

Water in Dermatoglyphics

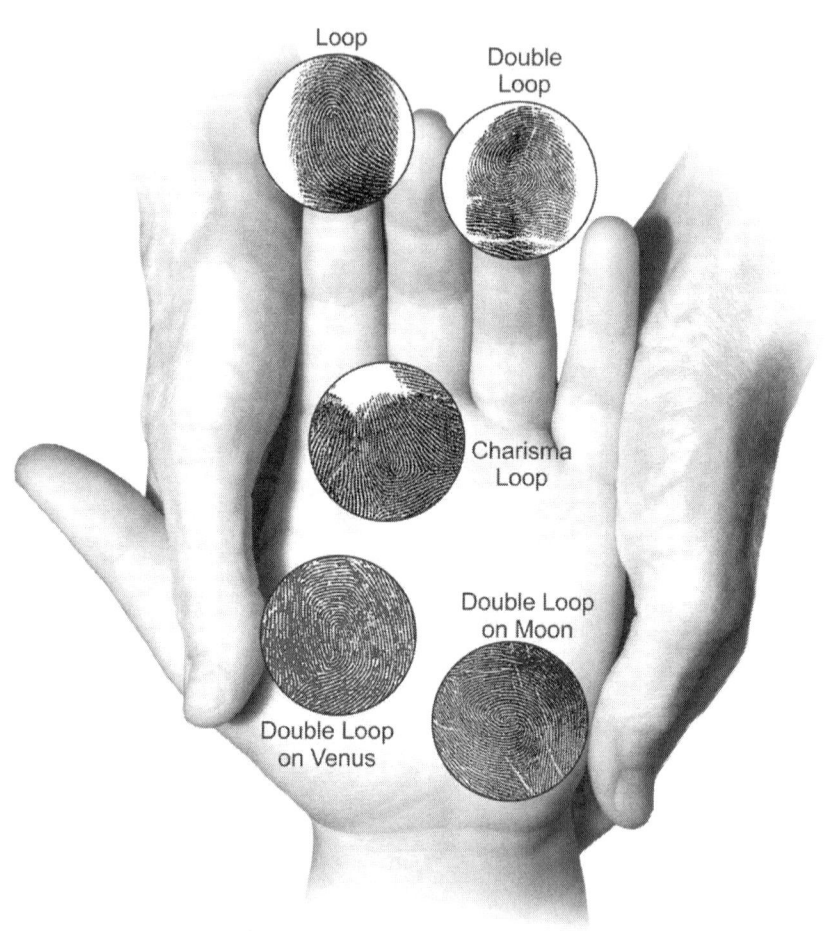

Charisma Loop - palmar

A loop drops downwards towards the wrist from between earth and water fingers. This glyph conjoins the steadfastness of the earth finger with the charm and self-confidence represented by the water finger. Also known as the 'rajah loop' in Indian palmistry. Owners may exude magnetism and personal authority.

Double Loop - digital

Like the yin yang, two loops intertwine, supported by a triradius on either side. Double loops signal sensitivity and intuition. Owners are judicial and diplomatic.

Double Loop on Moon - palmar

Two intertwined loops from a yin yang on a Moon mount. Judicial traits and masculine/feminine balance are aspected.

Double Loop on Venus - palmar

A double loop rests on a Venus mount. The excess water that is symbolized by the glyph adds to the earth governed mount and makes mud; traits of turbulent emotional duality and instability could present.

Loop - digital

The loop glyph flows in to recurve and exit on the same side of the fingertip. One triradius supports the loop. Loops look like a droplet of sensitive, fluid and cohesive water. Those with loops are adaptable, imaginative and responsive. Loops are the most common glyph.

Water in Dermatoglyphics

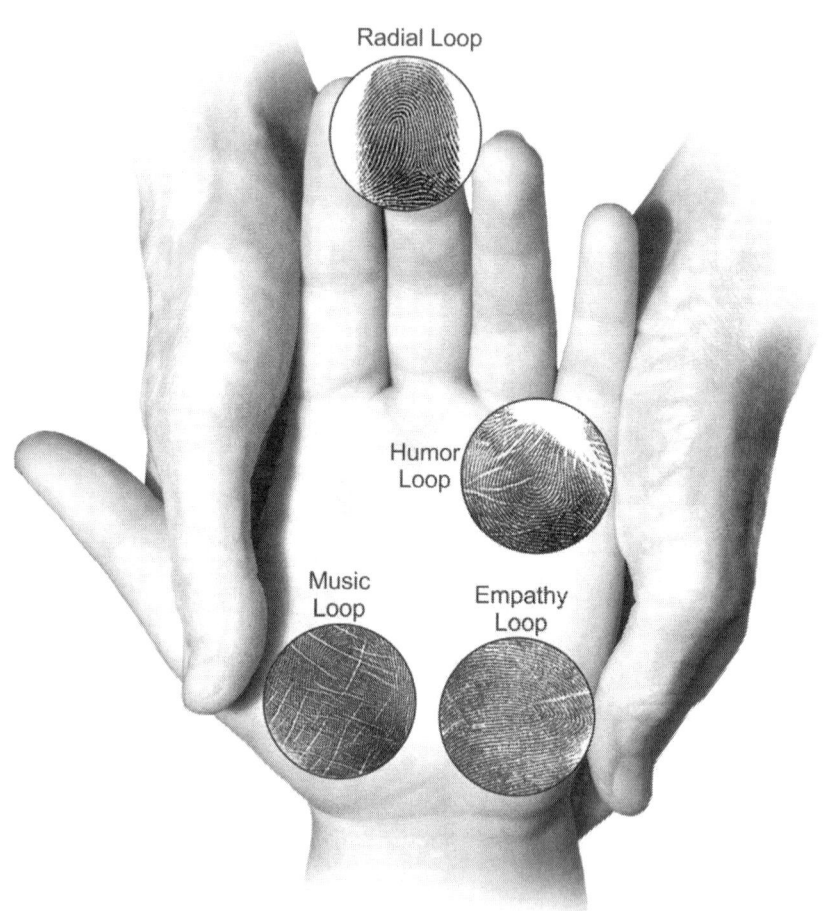

Empathy Loop on Moon - palmar

A loop flows in from the base of the palm, curves upwards over a Moon mount towards the ulnar side, then re-curves to stream out at point of entry.   Bearers are empathic, sensitive, nurturing and compassionate.

Humor Loop - palmar

A loop drops toward the wrist from between the air and fire fingers. The conjoining of compatible, upward lifting elements fire and air generate a light, expansive attitude, optimism, love of travel, humor that can be wry or run toward sarcasm or bitterness.

Music Loop on Venus - palmar

A large loop enters from the base of the thumb and flows upwards over a Venus mount. Love of music is assured; owners may or may not be musically gifted.

Radial Loop - digital

The ridges of radial loops enter from the radial side then recurves to exit on the same side of the fingertip. A radial loop opens to energy from the outer world and signals traits of adaptation, entrepreneurship, hyper-responsiveness to other's emotions and sensitivity to criticism.

Water in Dermatoglyphics

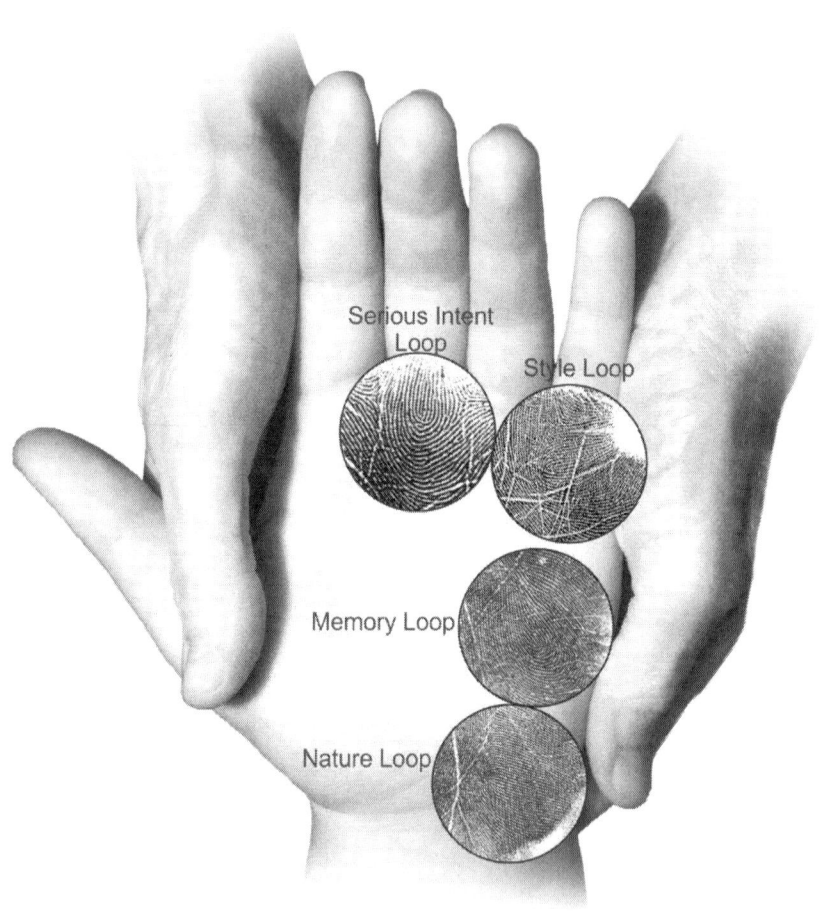

Memory Loop on Moon - palmar

A teardrop shaped loop flows onto the Moon mount from the radial side. People with memory loops are sensitive, imaginative and highly intuitive. Their long-term memory is more reliable than their short-term memory.

Nature Loop on Moon - palmar

A loop enters from the ulnar (baby finger) side of the palm, flows over the Moon mount and re-curves to outflow on the same side. Owners love nature and open spaces.

Serious Intent Loop - palmar

A loop drops downwards towards the wrist from between middle and ring fingers. The pattern unites the elements earth and fire to produce a drying, solidifying and stabilizing effect. Sense of responsibility and a sober work ethic is characterized.

Style Loop – palmar

A loop lies diagonally on a Sun mount underneath a fire finger. The watery loop's presence on the fiery Sun mount activates inspiration, imagination and design flair; style loops aspect admiration in the person of elegance and all things stylish.

Fire in Dermatoglyphics

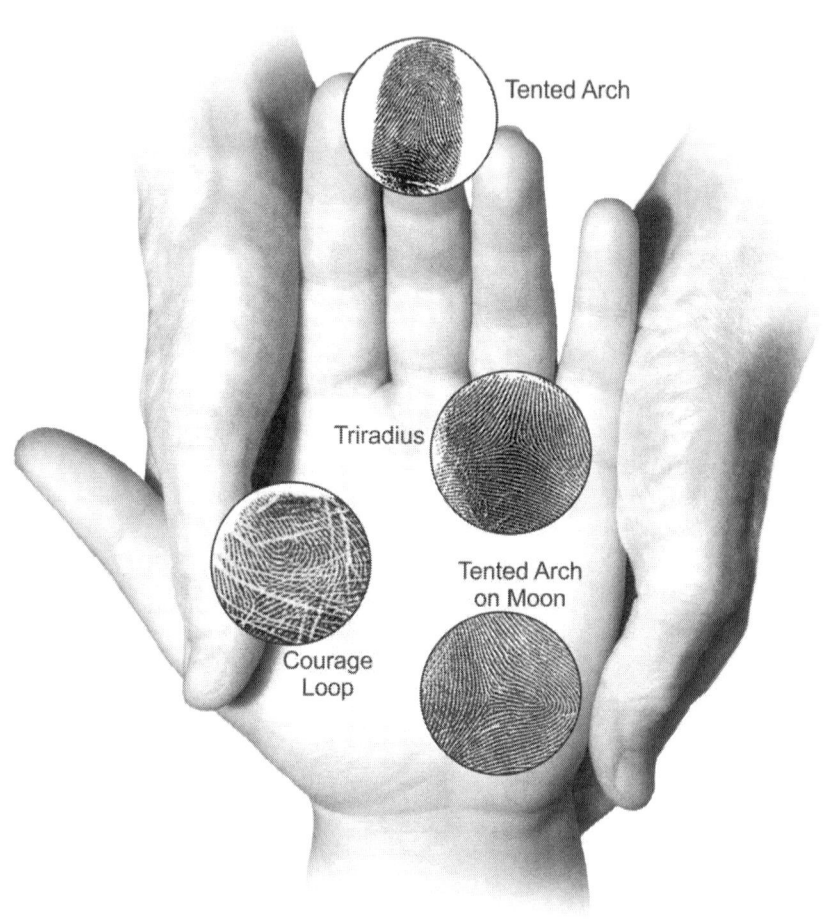

Courage Loop on Mars - palmar

A loop is embedded in a fire governed Mars mount between the beginning of the earth line and the protrusion of a thumb. Characteristics of energy, a warrior spirit and courage are ascribed to owners of this glyph.

Tented Arch - digital

Like a mountain with a volcano within, an arch drapes over a centrally positioned triradius. Fire is energetic and restless; owners might be highly strung, intense and enthusiastic.

Tented Arch on Moon - palmar

An arch drapes over a centrally positioned triradius on a Moon mount. This rarely found fire governed glyph suggests passion, enthusiasm, vitality and a sense of the dramatic.

Triradius - digital and palmar

Papillary ridges flowing from three directions converge to compose this three-pronged Y shaped pattern. While not defined as individual glyphs, the triradii appear on the palms. Additionally, their positions on digital dermatoglyphics determine the classification of the fingerprint into its category.

Air in Dermatoglyphics

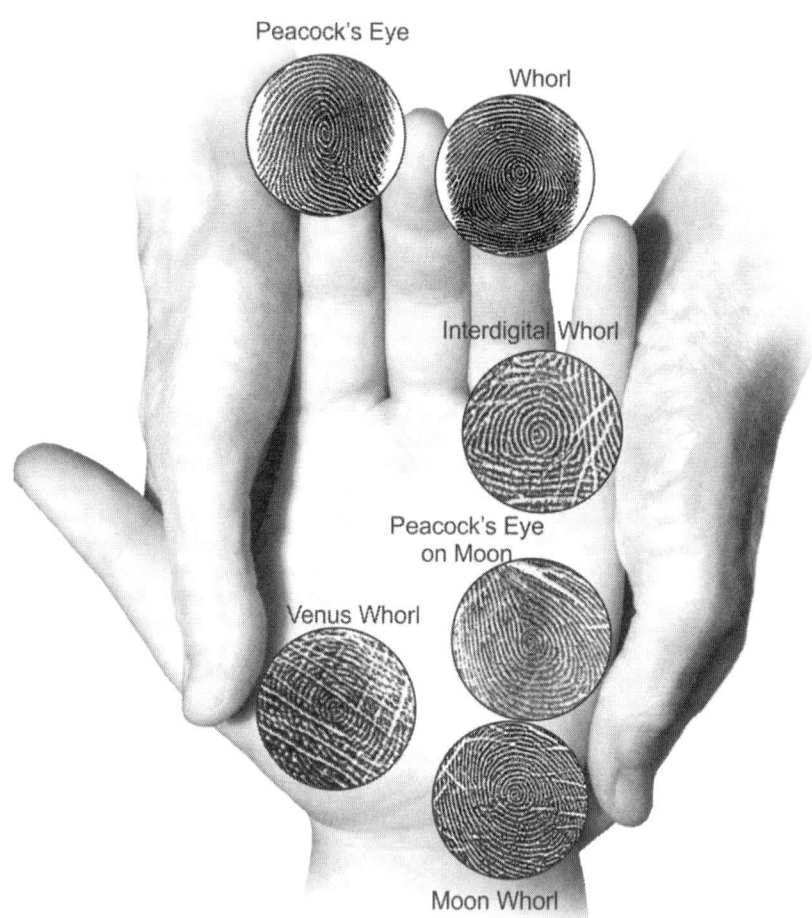

Peacock's Eye - digital

A loop contains a whorl in a teardrop shaped pocket, supported by one triradius. This exquisite glyph is traditionally said to bestow good fortune. Owners have a discerning eye, design flair, a high degree of power of observation and a developed sense of self preservation.

Peacock's Eye on Moon - palmar

A peacock eye pattern on a Moon mount is an added 'eye of perception' and is a definitive signal of intuition and creativity.

Whorl - digital

Whorls look like spirals or bull's eyes and have two triradii, one on either side. Principles of air include distance and curiosity. People with whorls are independent, analytical and individualistic.

Whorl, inter-digital - palmar

A small spiral is pocketed in a humor, serious intent or courage loop, signaling traits of curiosity, perceptiveness, individualism and detachment.

Whorl on Moon - palmar

A whorl on a Moon mount is like an air pocket that seeks separation from its emotional location; owners are creative and objective individualists who tend to emotionally detach.

Whorl on Venus - palmar

A whorl resting on an earth ruled Venus mount provides a circuit for exchange between sensual earth and curious air. Owners might have an unconventional or unusual lifestyle and an investigative interest in and understanding of all matters to do with sex.

- For in-depth interpretations of glyphs and their meanings, please refer to the publication "Chirology – Hand Reading – Palmistry – God Given Glyphs – Fingerprints".

Mounts

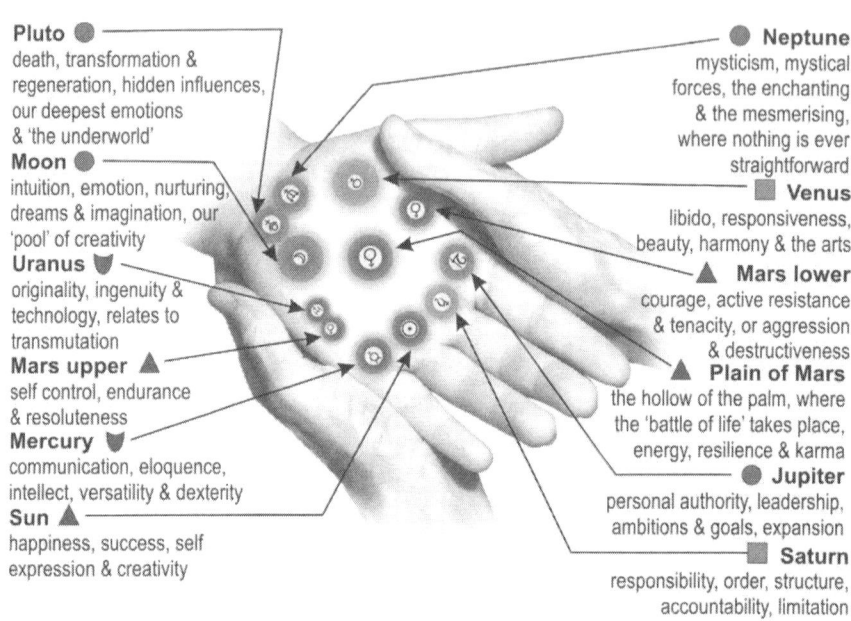

Pluto ●
death, transformation & regeneration, hidden influences, our deepest emotions & 'the underworld'

Moon ●
intuition, emotion, nurturing, dreams & imagination, our 'pool' of creativity

Uranus ♉
originality, ingenuity & technology, relates to transmutation

Mars upper ▲
self control, endurance & resoluteness

Mercury ☿
communication, eloquence, intellect, versatility & dexterity

Sun ▲
happiness, success, self expression & creativity

Neptune ●
mysticism, mystical forces, the enchanting & the mesmerising, where nothing is ever straightforward

Venus ■
libido, responsiveness, beauty, harmony & the arts

Mars lower ▲
courage, active resistance & tenacity, or aggression & destructiveness

Plain of Mars ▲
the hollow of the palm, where the 'battle of life' takes place, energy, resilience & karma

Jupiter ●
personal authority, leadership, ambitions & goals, expansion

Saturn ■
responsibility, order, structure, accountability, limitation

Mounts are the fleshy pads which contour over our palms. Each individual mount relates to and is a capacitor of different components of our human experience. We look at their comparative protrusion and fullness or deficiency; elasticity and springiness of the flesh adds resilience, while flatness or 'lifelessness' evidences depletion.

Sun/Apollo - fire - under fire fingers - happiness, creative self-expression, personal style, wealth, success, energy, talent, brilliance. **Saturn** - earth - under earth fingers - father, duty, responsibility, restriction

Jupiter - water - under water fingers - goals, ambition, leadership, possibility, expansion, capacity for out-reach, broader purpose, exposure, recognition, luck, achievement, personal authority

Mars Lower - fire - under the start of the earth lines, above the thumb's protrusion - courage, competitiveness, vitality, aggression

Plain of Mars - middle of hands - "where the battle of life take place"

Venus - earth - balls of the thumbs - libido, life force, vitality, sensuality

Neptune - water - base of palms between Venus and Moon/Pluto - dreams, intuition, mysticism

Pluto - water - under Moon - birth, death, degeneration, regeneration, rebirth, transformation, karma, the depths of the psyche, the primordial realms

Moon - water - fleshy pads on the ulnar sides of the hands - sensitivity, emotion, imagination, intuition, mother

Mars upper - fire - above Moon, below Mercury - determination, self-control, endurance

Uranus - air - above Moon, below Mercury - revolution, change, technology

Mercury - air - under air fingers - communication, versatility, dexterity

- For more about mounts, please see the publication "Palmistry – Signs & Symbols on the Mounts."

Digits ~ The 5 Identities

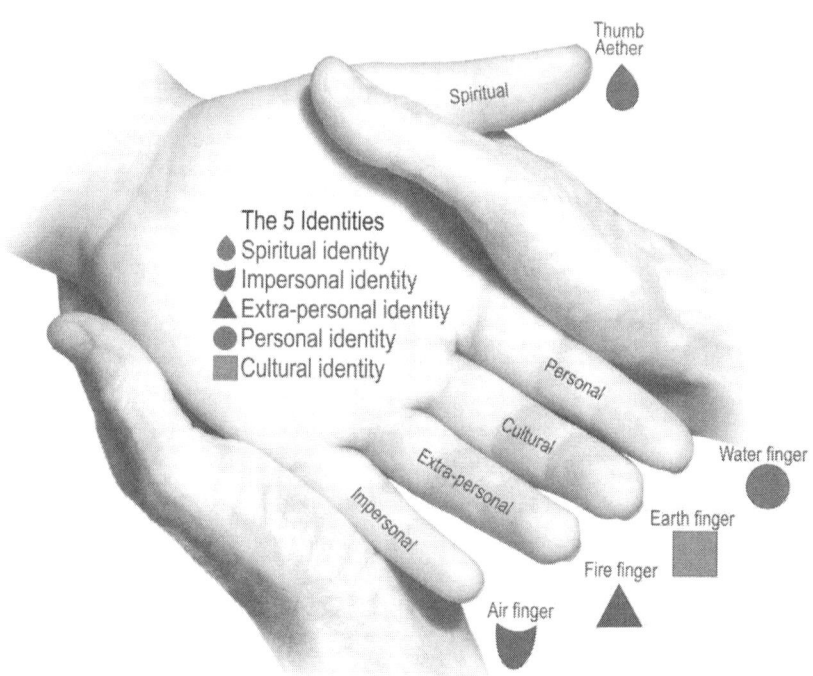

Thumb
Aether

Spiritual

The 5 Identities
- Spiritual identity
- Impersonal identity
- Extra-personal identity
- Personal identity
- Cultural identity

Personal

Cultural

Water finger

Extra-personal

Earth finger

Impersonal

Fire finger

Air finger

Fingers

The elements earth, water, fire, air and aether are individually ascribed to our 5 digits. Their length, relative lengths, breadth, flexibility, knottiness or smoothness, bends, leans, spaces between, lineal formations, set, glyphs, nails and placement of rings all yield information about orientations of thought. Each digit represents an area of life; these are termed the "5 Identities".

 Earth - cultural identity

Earth governed middle fingers relate to duty, discipline, structure, law and responsibility. They stand for formative familial and cultural influences and symbolize an inner point of balance.

 Water - personal identity

Water governed index fingers represent degree of self-worth and how we relate to and see ourselves.

 Fire - extra-personal identity

Fire governed ring fingers represent what we have to spare energetically, or not. Fire fingers represent creative self-expression, aesthetics and sport.

 Air - impersonal identity

Of our four fingers, air governed baby fingers have the most diverse array of associated interpretations. They aspect thought, communication, sexuality, business acumen and financial exchange.

 Aether - Spiritual Identity

In that we are the only beings with evolved thumbs, our aether governed fifth digits represent consciousness and our spiritual identity.

Knotty or Smooth

Knuckles that are noticeably wider than the phalanges above and below reveal a patient, detail oriented, analytical and philosophical thinker. Smooth fingers quicken the thought processes; thoughts are spontaneous and more intuitive.

Phalanges - Levels

The levels of our finger phalanges are each governed by an element; these are termed the "3 Worlds." They pertain to the material (water), executive (fire), and ideological (air) worlds respectively.

 Water level (basal) phalanges represent the foundation of our thinking. People with full basal phalanges look to the material world for security. Thin or waisted bases reveal the minimalist who might live in the realm of the intellect.

 Fire level phalanges are in the middle; they represent our mental response to administration and the execution thereof. Predominant fire level phalanges suggest practicality and orderliness. Aversion to administrative matters is more likely when this phalange level appears diminished.

 Air level phalanges are the tips of fingers. They represent our mental realm. Dominant tips show mental energy, the person finds security in thinking and conceptualizing.

Phalanges - individual

Each individual phalange stands for different potential skills and talents; chirologists observe if any stand out and predominate, or appear diminished in size.

Droplets

Little protuberances of flesh that look as if a drop of water could fall from the pad of the tip of the finger signify added receptivity and sensitivity, a tactile, sensual sense of touch and diplomacy.

Lines on Fingers

Vertical 'activation' lines on phalanges aspect mental hyper-activation and stress, especially if on the tips of all the fingers, while horizontal 'bar' lines suggest obstacles and blockages.

Grilles

Crisscross vertical and horizontal lines show areas of life where conflicts are experienced. For example, a grille on the water phalange of the water finger could indicate a troubled relationship with food; the person simultaneously restricts and desires food.

Setting

Set describes where the fingers sit on the hands; we assess the variables of levels from which the digits leave the palm.

Thick or Thin

Coping skills, materialism, practicality, robustness, energy and enjoyment of sex and food shows in thick fingers, while thin fingers belong to imaginative, idealistic, sensitive, less practical, frugal, fastidious, sexually reserved, fussy types.

Spacing

Ideally all fingers should be evenly spaced, but very often there are noticeable variables in space between each individual finger.

Bends

Bent fingers borrow energy from the adjacent finger and don't express themselves optimally. Fingers that bend inward to the palm want "to have and to hold". Air fingers that pull back show precision, fastidiousness and prudishness.

- For more about how to interpret fingers and thumbs, please refer to the publications "Chirology MANUAL - How to Read Hands." and "Illustrated Chirology Palmistry and Hand Reading."

Thumbs

Thumbs are governed by aether, the God principle; as one of the 5 Identities, they represent our 'spiritual identity'. Our thumbs are known as "the rulers of the hands" in all hand reading systems.

Their size, forms and markings modify interpretations for every other hand feature; they show measures of will power, strength of character, determination and ability to cope vs adaptive, passive resigned traits.

At least eleven criteria determine the strength or weakness of thumbs; lengths, breadths, set, angles of opening, relative lengths of the two phalanges, flexibility, dermatoglyphics, tip shapes, nail shapes, degrees of rotation and lineal markings.

- Small, thin thumbs reveal unassertive, sentimental traits, while long thick thumbs reveal energy, strength and determination.
- Bendy thumbs signal compliance; straight thumbs signal a
- resolute will.
- Thumb rings add physical weight to our most evolved digit, the person may feel depleted and in need of comfort and spiritual support.
- Angles of Dexterity are described by a masculine, squared and enlarged look to the joint at the base of thumbs; this feature shows a person who is good with their hands.
- Angles of Time and Harmony are formed by an angular or squared appearance to the bone at the very base of the thumb where the hand leaves the wrist; this feature associates with punctuality and a good sense of rhythm.
- Angles of Confidence are the angles from which our thumbs depart from our hands; they narrow and widen depending on how confident we are feeling in current time.

Nails

Assessment of nails is integral to every reading. Their four basic shapes each correspond to an individual element. Nail colors and formations are long known as windows to health; their condition is a front-line indicator for many diseases.

Shape
- Earth - small - narrow or square - slow to anger, slow to forget, materialistic, judgmental, argumentative, orderly
- Water - oblong - narrow - charming, idealistic, emotional
- Fire - fan-shaped - narrow base - broad top - restless, nervous, active, impatient
- Air - large - broad - open, frank, curious-minded, communicative

Color - traits
- Yellow - cranky, moody
- Pale - cool, restricted emotional expression
- Red - defensive, irritability, argumentativeness

Color - health
- Redness - high blood pressure
- White flecks - calcium or zinc deficiency, stress
- Blue around moons - respiratory, cardiovascular systems
- Brittle, cracked - skin condition - thyroid imbalance
- White and pale - anaemia, tiredness
- Concave or dished nails (spoon nail) - iron levels, lupus
- Ridges vertical - rheumatism, diabetes, thyroid
- Ridges horizontal (Beau's lines) - systemic trauma, infection
- Clubbed ('Hippocratic') - lungs, heart
- Brown/orange hues - kidneys, uric acid
- Yellow - liver

Nail biting

Shows worry, anxiety, stress, boredom, poor self-confidence, insoluble dilemmas with no resources, suppressed anger, reluctance to grow or to face the truth and deep inner loneliness.

- A set of fingers may have several differing nail shapes, in which case we relate that nail's features to the area of life represented by its finger.

- Nails that curve inwards towards the palms as they grow suggest challenging traits of insecurity, selfishness, and grasping possessiveness. Inward curves of fingers or nails say "it's all about me."

Client Information and Print Keeping

The beautiful value of palm prints is that they outlive us as sacred legacies of our unique personal signature. As professional chirologists, we find that our library of palm prints grows rapidly. For easy reference and follow up readings, we need a workable and accessible system by which to file our prints.

A computerized numerical record keeping method, whereby each set of prints is numbered and scanned then filed along with that person's information also works, but filing hard copies of the prints alphabetically into A4 lever arch files is a simple and recommended system.

Name: _____   Date: _____   Nr. _____

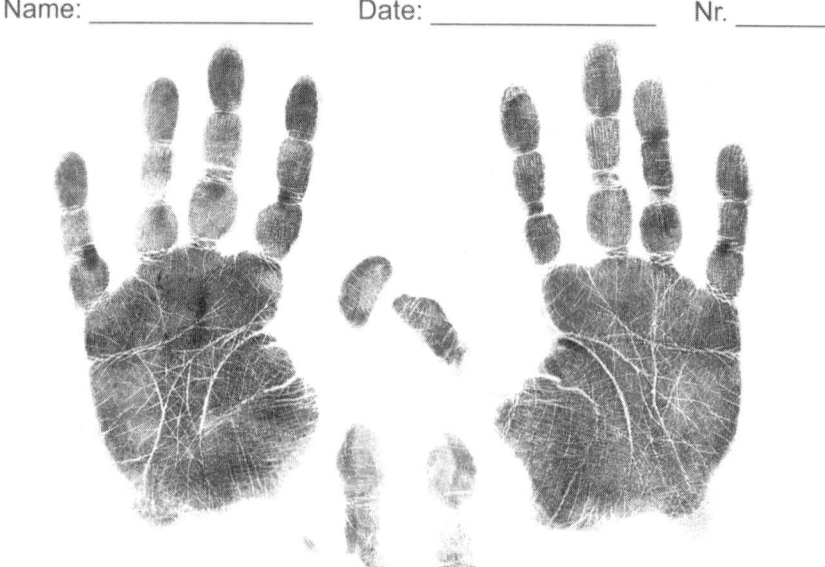

Ethics

Chirology is a diagnostic tool and healing modality that necessitates impeccable standards of ethical conduct. To meet and sustain professionalism, readers have a responsibility to adhere to set criterion of guiding principles. These include confidentiality, prohibiting distractions or interruptions and maintaining sexual and other boundaries. We ensure that there is no ambiguity regarding the fee for the session. We tell our clients that chirology is not prediction and fortune telling and explain that chirology is a dialogue therapy and that they'll benefit most optimally if they participate in the conversation.

For me personally, there have been several times over the years where I've rejected a potential client. Those who insist they want prediction must seek elsewhere. The same applies for those who, on the phone, come across as being unstable or high, or where I intuitively know to refer them elsewhere. I've had to find my no.

Some situations are way beyond our scope of practice. An extreme example of this is a WhatsApp message I once received from a man asking for a consultation in which he informed me "I am addicted to drugs, sex and sin. I am a murderer and I am sure I am demonically possessed." Needless to say, I had to protect myself. I referred him to Narcotic Anonymous and blocked him. This situation would have tested my personal emotional limitations and physical safety as well as tested ethics related to confidentiality.

Your glance at a set of hands will often, in a flash of intuitive perception, reveal highly accurate information about that person, but never proffer any opinions unless the person has asked. An unsolicited hand (or other) reading is an extremely annoying violation of privacy.

Readers and therapists who become sexually intimate with their clients or patients are abandoning their client's and their own deeper needs. Palm readers who mess with seduction are creepy charlatans; they break trust and degrade and damage the authenticity of our craft. Like with all professional therapies, the ethical responsibility of the chirologist is to keep impeccable sexual boundaries.

.

Water

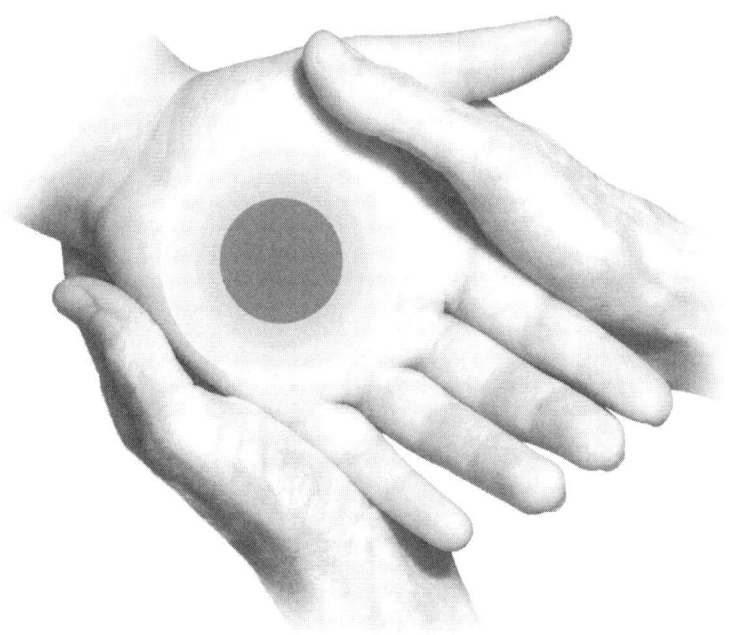

Texture ~ Connection

WATER ~ TEXTURE ~ CONNECTION

Counseling

"A problem shared is a problem halved." Englsh Proverb.

Basic counseling know-how is an essential ingredient in the hand reader's tool kit. The counseling process is a confidential conversation which provides support and guidance for the client's life situation. In assisting clients to find the source of the problems that are causing mental and emotional distress, counselors facilitate self-awareness. Generally, the focus is on issues that are rooted in past trauma.

Sitting face to face, the dialogue opens for those concerns which are in the heart and mind of the client to enter into the soul of the counselor, who provides a respectful and non-judgmental space that is dedicated to their client's self-acceptance, personal growth, healing and integration.

Counseling differs from coaching in that while most coaching models are solution oriented towards attainment of desired goals, counselors facilitate the bringing of memories to the light of consciousness. Attention is paid to feelings and to the externalization of internalized emotions. With the use of various applications of psychological theory, technique and process, emphasis in counseling is also on improvement of both subjective and outward communication. Counselors strive to optimize their client's inner guidance compass, encourage behavior change, and improve self-esteem.

Counselors are trained to respect their client's values. The client is offered unconditional positive regard; the issues they bring to counseling are seen as the problem, not the person. The benefits of counseling are relative to the client's willingness to self-inquire. Depending on circumstances, the therapeutic duration varies from short to long-term; patients can be in therapy for months, years or even decades.

Coaching

"The meeting of two personalities is like the contact of two chemical substances. If there is any reaction, both are transformed."   Carl Jung

Coaching is collaborative and empowering conversation that assists clients to discover their own answers and take ownership of their inner resources. The focus of various coaching models differs.

Conventional coaching is goal-orientated, often targeting high professional performance.   Focus is on motivation, self-determination and attainment of objectives. Coaches encourage realistic behavioral strategies that unlock and maximize personal development, for example, the positive psychology approach of using self-talk to affirm the opposite of negative beliefs and to "let them go". With the use of various methods and techniques, coaches hold the client accountable for carrying out agreed upon action steps towards goal attainment.

Life coaching processes that are harmonious with the 5 Realm model of counseling and coaching with chirology are those which are centered in present time experience. Now centered coaching styles include goal-focused conventional coaching, but place emphasis on inviting clients to disengage from their storyline, to drop in to the aether governed realm of the eternal now and to share limiting beliefs, fears and emotions.

In holding empathic presence and with supportive enquiry questions, now-centered coaches simultaneously aid clients to sustain a somatic awareness of the physical sensations that are occurring in their bodies, to sense into their nervous systems and their feelings, and to "surf their emotions." Discomforts and uncertainties are held in a sacred space that allows for what is showing up to "be there". From this place of open vulnerability, clients are empowered to optimally reframe situations, explore possibilities and decide on action steps that will improve the trajectory of their lives.

Counseling and Coaching with Chirology

"Until you make the unconscious conscious,
it will direct your life, and you will call it fate."
Carl Jung

Chirology is the only dialogue therapy modality where specifically the hands are held; we reassuringly hold and stroke people's hands, look closely, and sense for intuitive perceptions that arise and refer to the hand prints which inform and direct us to the situation. The intimate and personal nature of the craft of interpreting the shapes, skin textures, mounts, lines, glyphs and other features of the hands is a powerful point of departure into the seeker's psyche which rapidly takes both client and reader into deep emotional, mental and spiritual waters. Chirologists endeavor to create an integrative and transformative experience for their clients. In lending full presence, we gather, and attend to their story. We rapidly identify the component parts of current time issues and past; the who, why, how and what has happened and what is happening in their lives.

The chirological process is composed of three primary components. First is an interpretive system, which in the context of this book is the 5 element system with its 5 Realm counseling and coaching model. The second component is intuition, and the third is the least spoken of and researched area of the hand reading modality; the how-to of verbal delivery.

With the use of the of the 5 Realm model as our essential counseling and coaching infrastructure, palm reading evolves into an alchemical dialogue therapy. We draw our counseling and coaching techniques from psychology and from both now-centered and goal focused coaching methods. Additionally, readers are free to include other support methods, modalities and alternative divinatory tools.

Using the combination of interpretation of the forms and features of the hands with skilled incorporation of selected counseling and coaching methods, we perceive our client's sub-conscious and conscious coping mechanisms and their needs and preferences.

For the client, the sharing of their story with a trustworthy person relieves, lightens the load, gives perspective and accelerates self-understanding. The offering of a few considered and insightful observations about their hand's features reassures; the client soon feels safe enough to participate in the sharing of their story. Alchemy is in the telling, but while the initial telling of the story is an imperative, if the person is stuck in the story forever, then transformation is unlikely. Their growth edge relies on subjective communication. Are they open to explore the somatic, to connect with where they hold feelings in their body?

As readers, we facilitate for clients to feel their feelings and to pay attention to their longings, which have feelings behind them (I'm sad, there is a longing behind it). The more space the reader allows for feelings, the closer the client comes to the essence of the situation. Readers who guide clients into the somatic, to sense into where in the body they store complexities of emotional fibers, will help fast-track healing. We want the telling of their story to facilitate their getting their brains out of the way, then to establish and maintain communication with their authentic emotions.

The vulnerable and open setting requires professional navigation and sensitive guidance from the reader. The 5 Realms provide context, content and a safety net. By the end of the reading, the client has a more cohesive sense of how well they are doing (or not) in each of the respective realms and their constituent parts. This structured approach ensures that the reading is not a random hit and miss affair.

Intuition

"The only real valuable thing is intuition."
Albert Einstein

With the advent of remote viewing as a recognized science, we have in collective consciousness an unprecedented validation of the power of our "inner tuition'. Gut feelings, hunches and sixth senses are always alive in the background of our interface with life; whether or not we consciously accept or recognize it, our intuition pervades our lives. Intuition comes before thought and is like listening from beneath the surface. Information that has nothing to do with intellect and analysis arises from an indefinable source; we experience a certainty of knowing that is more senior than belief.

Chiromancy, the aether governed, divinatory realm of chirology, describes our intangible capacity for intuitive perception and channelling. The term comes from Greek 'kheri', meaning hand, and Latin 'mantei/mantic', defined as having to do with divination, or the act of foreseeing the future, or telling of the unknown, by inspiration, by magic, or by signs and omens. Inextricably enmeshed with chirology, our resonance calibrating faculties are like binding threads that interweave with the entire hand reading experience. When we are in attuned awareness, our portals of perception open to impressions that arise as images, messages, metaphors, colors, physical sensations, tastes and smells.

Our hands "speak", they exude differing frequencies of energy; subtle nuances radiate from amidst the palmar lines and patterns, but contrary to popular belief, the information the hands emanate is often not directly indicated in their forms and markings. Some psychically gifted hand readers do use the old fatalistic Indian and Gypsy tradition of looking for one marking to foretell the specific number of children or length of life and are able, sometimes with astonishing accuracy, to describe past, present and future situations, but it cannot be verified that any predicted, psychic or clairvoyant information comes directly from the hands as such.

The quest to deepen sensitivity to and trust in our intuitive and psychic capacities is a prevailing theme for most hand readers, the how to of feeling into and trusting the quality of information that downloads from non-material realms. Keen intuition refines with holding and looking at many sets of hands, from being close to and reading the hands of many people. Psychic and intuitive perceptiveness can be further developed with cultivating mindfulness, with grounding in the "natural great peace" of meditation, with prayer, with listening from our deepest levels through all our senses, and through the many available psychic development courses offered by professionals.

Paradoxically, the more we learn and practice chirology's scientific system, we simultaneously develop a capacity to set aside our technical know-how and learn to think beyond our thoughts. With observation, listening, and making constant cross references of association, intuition develops along with the capacity for the self-trust required to verbally and energetically channel and articulately share the impressions.

Generally, unless very certain of the accuracy of your insights, it is advisable to avoid prediction of specific and exact outcomes, but clients rely on our intuition. When we hold back from sharing what might be crucial information, they will unconsciously experience disappointment.

Consider too that even when what is said by the reader is inaccurate, that this might activate a heightened clarity for the client about what for them is their best course of action. Don't lose the opportunity that presents in the moment of inspiration; allow the sacred soul self to work, be courageous and speak out directly. Trust yourself. What you tell them is what they need to hear.

- Spheres of psychic skills include clairaudience (hearing sounds, voices and messages), clairvoyance (visual images), clairsentience (felt senses in the body), claircognizance (overall psychic 'knowing'), extra-sensory perceptions (sixth sense, reception of information not gained through physical senses), retrocognition (knowledge of a past event), precognition (knowledge of the future), telepathy (thought transference), remote viewing (receiving mental impressions about a distant or unseen target), psychometry (information yielded by a material item) and telekinesis (ability to influence physical matter without physical interaction)

Chirology is Now Centered

The conversation in chirology includes identifying past events, but we do like to emphasize current time; how well is the person doing 'here and now'? The optimal approach is the enquiry into the effects of past events and whether or not they are consciously or unconsciously affecting the person in present time. Impactful events are retained as markings in the hands, but the event itself is not happening in present reality.

In the same way, predicting future events, dates and outcomes on behalf of another person is disempowering and of little value to the client, who has free will to change their attitudes towards past, present and anticipated future experience. Prediction side-tracks us from exploring a more empowering awareness; our attitudes and beliefs co-create our present experience and influence our future.

In traditional palmistry, emphasis is often on identifying past events and situations and on prediction of future outcomes. When an intuitive hand reader correctly times and describes a past scenario, clients are excited and impressed. They feel understood and rapport and trust immediately deepen. But while accelerated rapport between reader and client is immensely beneficial, the identification of the event in and of itself does little to facilitate the client's growth.

We support clients by helping them to clarify their needs and preferences and then, in co-creation with existence, to harness the tools of desire, imagination and expectancy that optimally potentize future outcomes.

Our subjective vibrational frequency determines destiny far more powerfully than somebody else's perception of a fated, cast in stone future. We have a timeline, our story, our dream of the future and the present moment.

The moment has no duration, we are always now, in timelessness. Perceptions, of past events, and the patterns that create future events, can and do change.

In the context of what we think about comes about, discussions are qualitative and within a holistic paradigm. Rather than chronological evaluation of the person, it is to the now, to how they are in the present; that we most attend.

Rapport

In professional counselling or coaching relationships, the quality of the alliance between the counselor and the client is key to their collaboration. As important as the reader's expertise is the establishing of connection. In the hand reading context, the significance of rapport is intensely highlighted. As dialogue therapists, by deepening our understanding of the element style of communication that the client best grasps and responds to, the quality and style of our delivery can be optimally refined. Here are some suggestions for establishing a basis for rapport:

- Ready the consultation space before the client arrives. Create a harmoniously restful ambiance. Have water, tissues, your recording device and client information and indemnity forms ready for them to fill in. Have your ink printing materials ready in advance, along with soap and a towel for washing. Warm the room if necessary.
- Do a subjective check-in around feelings you as a reader may have about the client, and be sure to manage the feelings.
- Set aside personal situations, problems and issues for the duration of the client's visit.
- Present with an air of being calm, prepared and un-rushed.
- When they arrive, shake their hand, seat and orientate them to where the reading will be held.
- Perhaps ask how they found you, who referred.
- Explain a little of the structure of what they might expect. Tell them that the conversation is confidential and that this is their time, their investment in themselves.
- Be receptive and open to any questions they might ask.
- Ask what they hope to get out of the reading. What brings them? Have they had readings before? Have they been in therapy? How much self-inquiry have they done?
- Explain about the palm printing, how it works.

Rapport with Earth Types

Earth dominant type people are self-reliant and seldom seek readings. Consider the behavior of earth in nature; earth is fixed and is the only element that doesn't move unless it is moved. When counseling and coaching clients who present with many earth governed features in their hands, this principle of immovability is an important criterion.

Self-analysis and emotional excavation are not natural defaults, instead an innate stability, calmness and freedom from persistent negative feelings is characterized. Feelings and bad memories are buried and aren't easily shared. Attempts to excavate, to dig deeply into and disturb their psyche may well be met with resistance. Unless the discussion is practical, earth people might seem rather unwilling or unable to open up.

To gain rapport with and to optimally support people with many earth governed features in their hands, explain some practical earth principles; the concepts will appeal to their fundamental pragmatism. Help them to open, connect with and share their core feelings by speaking slowly, simply and methodically. Convey your interpretation using structured explanations. Give them time to ruminate, deliberate, understand and integrate what it is you are sharing. Offer reassurance. Be gentle and authentic. Go at their pace.

Earth Governed Features in Hands
- Earth shaped hands with square palms and short fingers
- Rough skin
- Stiffness in the consistency of the hands adds earth
- Very few lines
- Short air lines
- Arch dermatoglyphics

Rapport with Water Types

As is the case with each of the archetypes, our overview of all the features of the person's hands helps us to optimally adapt our communication style. When counseling and coaching a water type person, consider that their subjective experience is sensitive, emotional and sensory; rather than intellectually defining their thoughts, they receive impressions of the sense of an idea, or the feeling it evokes.

Water dominant people respond best to intimate, gentle, quiet and empathic dialogue; don't be overbearing. Avoid anything loud, harsh or coarse. Be very personal, emphasize your understanding of their subjectivity, of how they experience life internally. Affirm their sensitive interface with life. They come seeking supportive kindness, not clever rhetoric. They'll feel assaulted by a barrage of analytical theory (suited more to the air type) or hard, fast and cutting-edge sentences (suited more to fire types).

Water Governed Features in Hands
- Long slender hands with oblong palms and long fingers
- Soft moist skin
- Flexible hands with soft consistency
- Wavy air lines
- Thin, delicate lines
- Upper minor water lines
- Puffy mounts
- Large Moon mounts
- Loop dermatoglyphics
- Flexible thumbs

Rapport with Fire Types

When fire displays as the person's primary temperament, your willingness to facilitate changes and adjustments in their life will be valued. Fire energy in hands shows a quick thinker, a person whose thoughts are objective and rational. They are logical and will appreciate cognitive facts and practical advice. To sustain optimal rapport and keep the attention of someone with fire shaped hands, the best delivery style is straight, to the point, clear and precise.

Present concepts systematically; easily irritated fire dominant types may tend towards challenging the reader argumentatively, with forceful expression. Speak with authority about scientific principles and engage tested coaching techniques. Be organized; define your points sharply and specifically. Punctuate your sentences expressively, and do not speak too slowly. These people are easily bored and will enjoy being met with a sparky, energetic style of dialogue.

Fire Governed Features in Hands
- Fire shaped hands with oblong palms and short fingers
- Roughish skin texture with visible pores, skin ridges can be felt
- Dry skin
- Small hands, especially if also firm
- Firm hands
- Straight lines
- Rising lines
- Fire lines clear and strong
- Well-developed Mars mounts
- Tented arch dermatoglyphics
- Wide set thumbs

Rapport with Air Types

To optimize rapport with someone with many air features, it is recommended that hand readers develop their vocabulary. It is the air influence that aspects the talkative communicator who enjoys sophisticated eloquence and interesting, lively dialogue.

Be the articulate communicator; it is with air archetype clients that we can share something of the principles of chirology; the why and how the markers in their hands have meanings will interest them.

Many air features in a set of hands reveal a curious, analytical and philosophical person who seeks answers to why things are the way they are. They are motivated by understanding and can see a wide range of perspectives. The person is conceptual and interested in impartial truth. Air types have personal viewpoints and could be given to interrupting you as a reader to get their opinion across.

Air Governed Features in Hands
- Air shaped hands with square palms and long fingers
- Smooth, dry skin
- Fingers held wide when speaking
- Many lines
- Long air lines
- Minor air lines
- Large Mercury mounts
- Whorl dermatoglyphics
- Knotty fingers

Touching and Holding

Spontaneously taking another person's hands, whether to shake, play, or console is a natural gesture that connects us. This is already a good reason to look a little closer into the importance of touch in the work of hand reading. The benefits of the skilled holding of another's hands cannot be underestimated; our therapeutic touch has a pivotal role. In lovingly holding and stroking people's hands, we offer them validation, acceptance, appreciation, and more.

Touch first happens when the client arrives; we shake hands. For the printing process, we again take their hands and stroke their skin so as to assess skin texture. At the beginning of the reading, when we first properly and confidently receive their hands in ours, a more powerful connection occurs. With our holding and stroking, a force of energies intertwine, connectivity is established, the client feels safe and reassured, and the courageous leap into self-enquiry via the hands' forms and markings begins. Through touch, both reader and seeker open and extend themselves.

After some minutes, and once initial rapport is established, letting go of the person's hands will feel comfortable, natural and appropriate. From time to time throughout the reading it will feel right to again ask for their hands, perhaps to with pen or pointed crystal point out a marking, or to comfort them, or to look for more markers that exude messages for you as the reader to convey.

As you draw the reading to a close and if it feels comfortable and right, hold their hands in yours again for the recommended suggestion for how to end readings.

Sexuality

Eye contact and the holding of hands along with generous empathic listening make for an exceptionally close and intimate experience. Spontaneous sexual attraction is, at some stage in the career of a chirologist, inevitable. Attraction happens; this may be mutual, or more commonly is felt on the part of the client, who might begin to try to touch you back, or seduce you in some other way.

Variations of sexual energy or innuendo are best managed professionally by the reader through being light, smiling, offering a few words of respectful, wisely articulated acknowledgement of the attraction, and then skillfully guiding the conversation back to the real reason for the person wanting the consultation.

Some clients are insistently seductive, which can be very distracting and draining. In these situations, the reader could try to keep a sense of humor and do their best to diffuse, redirect the focus and move on with the reading. Another avenue to explore might be to use this experience to open the conversation into matters to do with the client's sexuality.

Crying

In a dialogue therapy practice, three variables present; the client cries, the client and reader cry together, or the reader cries.

When the floodgates open for a client, don't be in any hurry to move on. Physiologically speaking, both happy and sad tears are self-regulating; they come when a person's system shifts from sympathetic to parasympathetic activity, from a state of high tension and arousal to a period of recalibration, relative calmness and recovery. That they are willing and able to be with you in this way means that something worthwhile is happening. Flowing tears are a useful, meaningful and positive affirmation of emotional processing. A spot has been touched, this calls for readers to relax, pause and do nothing except hold presence, to allow space for the client to share what arises in them.

Immediately reaching to take their hands, hug, pat, offer tissues or ask questions such as "why are you crying?" are over-reactive responses which are generated by the reader's own anxious desire to fix. Comments like "what's wrong?" or "there's no need to cry about it!" or "everything will be fine!" are unhelpful, they negate, delegitimize and weaken rapport.

Once the emotions subside, we do take their hands in ours again, and ask the enquiry question: "What is the thought that helped you cry?" This question may elicit more healing tears. Notice that we ask "what helped" rather than "why are you crying?" Asking about the thoughts, images and recollections that brought on the tears evokes authentic feelings and minimizes their retreat into far less useful intellectual analysis.

When we readers are moved to tears and cry along with our clients, it might be that our own personal issues are triggered by their situation, that their struggles parallel ours, but our responses must be delicately tuned to the client's needs. It is okay for therapists to be vulnerable, but are we enacting countertransference and crying more for ourselves? Especially if the client is themselves a caregiver who is attuned to others' needs, our crying will overwhelm, unsettle and distance them.

Views on mutual emotional release in the therapeutic context differ, but it could also be that in some situations, our crying together communicates a strong connection and a deeply empathic response that does not distract. Instead, the client's seeing us emotional might mean a lot to them; through this lens our mutual tears draw us closer, cement rapport, reinforce our shared humanity, and communicate that we are listening, caring and maximally attuned.

Generally speaking, therapists are cautioned against crying; we ought to be like a blank slate, our crying will distract, turn the focus and make the situation about us instead of about the client. But in the context of a long-term professional practice where we see many clients, there might arise one or two memorable occasions when on hearing the client's story, unmanageable emotion arises and we are moved to tears.

This situation is uncomfortable; there is concern as to how the grief affects the client, with efforts to suppress the tears that threaten to overwhelm. But perhaps tears are a visual testament of our humanity that communicate caring and understanding more powerfully than words could. Therapists do occasionally cry when working with clients; when we lose boundaries in this way, we can but be friendly to our feelings and offer forgiving tenderness and compassion for our imperfect selves.

Rescuing

"Trying to fix a person leaves them rejected in their being."
Kåre Landfald

While the urge to help is sourced in our beginningless goodness and is an essentially pure expression of compassion, wanting to fix could well arise from fear; I am not comfortable with my own emotions, therefore I will try to fix yours. When effortfully trying to resolve a problem on behalf of a client, we are functioning at the vibrational level of the problem itself.

Watch for the tendency to want to rescue. Aspire to leave the person, who may not be ready to change, completely in their own business. Bearing witness, being present to their pain, is enough. Become less and less attached to results on their behalf. We are not responsible for analytically figuring things out for them; the less ambition to direct them to a solution, the better the results. The solution is to stop looking for the solution. In our role as dialogue therapists, we are advised to serve without goals or attachment to results.

By way of practicing non-attachment, keep half of your attention and awareness subjective, within yourself. Cultivate cool love, be accepting, be interested, but without an agenda. Listen from the heart with compassion and empathy rather than with emotional sympathy. Inclusion, embrace and deeply present listening to what IS for the person, is what goes to their core.

Children ~ Couples ~ Families

Since analysis of children's hands is at the request of the parents, the question is whether to sit with the child personally or whether to report to the parent. Much depends on their age, the situations at hand and on how proficient you as a reader feel about working with a child, adolescent or teen.

Younger children relate well when consultations are interactive. Together we draw in their lines with colored pencils. I've found that when I offer broad explanations of the relevance of a line or fingerprint, that kids become very curious. It then becomes easy to let them lead the conversation with their questions. Through affirming their stronger attributes, they might feel safe to share what is in their heart. From age 8 – 14 or so, it is probably best to consult with both parent and child together. If we discuss the child without their being present, the child might feel compromised; this should be clarified and defined before we take the palm prints.

For the most part, children and teens love having their hands read. For older teens, our mutual exploration of their preferences and potential vocational aptitudes gives them a safe space and a voice. Chirology readings for teenagers are significantly helpful for subject choice for high school and college.

Dysfunctional patterns between couples and family members have complicated and diverse roots and dynamics. Whether we read for two people in one session or for individuals in separate consultations, couples and family counseling takes us into deep waters. This special skill set is somewhat beyond the scope of chirology. Working with couples and families requires being an objectively unbiased observer but this is very difficult to sustain; we easily feel more sympathetic to and identified with one person over another.

The question of whether one therapist should work with both people in a couple's relationship or with all members in a family constellation is an old debate; many professionals prefer to see one person only and refer others to different therapists.

Nevertheless, chirology is a powerful aid that helps those who struggle in relationships to better understand themselves and each other. Through the hands and dialogue, the quality of love and commitment between people can be readily assessed, along with their respective love languages and where needs and expectations aren't being met. An empathic reader rapidly picks up on the clients' feelings, such as resentment, anger, pain and mistrust, which may or may not yet have been admitted or articulated. With couples, whether one wants divorce and the other doesn't, is soon identified. If the relationship seems salvageable, the reader mediates to help them deepen their union with better communication, goal setting and compromise.

Some readers are drawn to and feel an affinity with using chirology to counsel and coach couples and families. For this complex and specialized field; readers are advised to undergo separate training to further qualify themselves.

Supportive Modalities and Referrals

Chirology marries well with astrology, runes, numerology, tarot and other divinatory tools. My personal favorites that I incorporate in readings are runes, tarot and astrology, each of which open new portals. Physiognomy, kinesiology, NLP (Neuro Linguistic Programming) and hypnotherapy are other recommended support modalities, as are those listed below. Enjoy the options, the flexibility, and the diversity. Referring clients to other therapists up-levels competence; growing a list of practitioners to refer to is recommended.

Cognitive Behavioral Therapy (CBT)

This is a solution focused therapy that blends well with other therapies. It uses tools, tasks and strategies to identify problem issues and core beliefs to positively change dysfunctionally reactive behavioral patterns. CBT It is a particularly effective approach for anxiety and depression based disorders.

Emotional Freedom Techniques (EFT)

EFT is a dynamic, scientifically researched and tested applied energy technology that combines tapping on specific meridian acupressure points with dialogue. Used either as a self-help tool or in consultation with an EFT practitioner, tapping on specific issues induces positive changes in our biochemistry. Stress hormones reduce and feel good hormones increase. After a few rounds of tapping, the emotional intensity of the situation neutralizes. If the client is a willing participant in learning the sequence, they will receive a deeply effective somatic experience of what is happening now. Using EFT in a chirology consultation is highly recommended.

Eye Movement Desensitization and Reprocessing Therapy (EMDR)

As an interactive psychotherapy technique that fast-tracks emotional and mental healing, EMDR involves the use of eye movements. Different aspects of traumatic memories are focused on while clients simultaneously focus on the external stimulus of visually tracking the therapist's hand as it moves back and forth across their field of vision. Distress associated with past and current experiences is cognitively re-framed. EMDR is recognized as a highly effective treatment for trauma, PTSD, anxiety and depression.

Family Constellation Therapy

As the name implies, this therapy is designed to help identify unrecognized inter-generational familial dynamics that influence our current lifetime. We have invisible psychical loyalties attaching us to often unknown ancestral traumas, such as deaths and suicide, abuse, violence and war. The therapy draws from indigenous spiritual mysticism; connection with ancestors is intrinsic to a constellation process. The interactive therapy involves the appointing of others or symbols to stand as proxy for family members. The experience is supportive; in the quantum of the morphic field, both seeker and participating representatives feel an alive and emotionally empathic connectivity with the seeker's historical and current disharmonies.

Supervision

We readers are keepers of frequency; we hold space for the most disturbingly traumatic of life stories. From the oppressed to the privileged. our practice is infused with multi-dimensional diversity; we interface with clients from every walk of life, from every age, situation and orientation. In service to others and with aspirational intent, we do our utmost best with each client, yet challenging consultations and situations, where we reach impasses or disruptions, are inevitably going to occur. Additionally, we serve as role models regarding openness to self-exploration, but our deep conversations intermingle with the subjective influences of our personal values, attitudes, beliefs and bias. How do we keep up-levelling our professional competency, knowledge and skill?

Supervision, a collaborative relationship with a person who is experienced in both therapy and supervision, has a facilitative and evaluative function that is aimed at refining the strategies and skills used by the therapist. Required of trained, qualified and licensed therapists, supervision is designed to monitor the quality of the service provided.

Thoughtful, transparent dialogue and open discussion with another counselor or coach of what happens consciously and unconsciously in readings alerts us to our own shadow emotions. Shadow resides in the unconscious and plays out in devious ways; with supervision we minimize clouded perceptions and interference from subjective feeling states. By reaching out and asking someone to assume a supervisory role, we receive support, learn, and enhance professional competence.

Fire

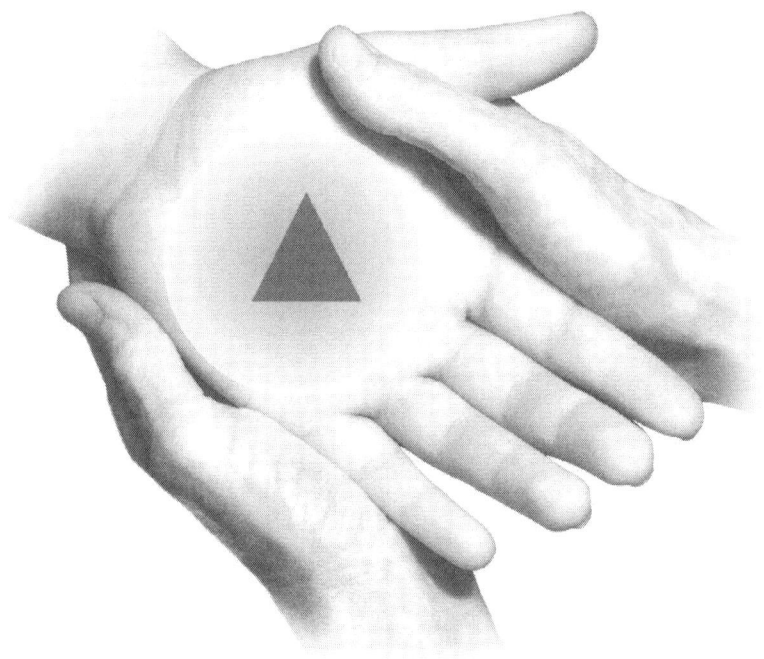

Color ~ Fuel

FIRE ~ COLOR ~ FUEL

Themes ~ Life's Situations and Experiences

In this section, I've presented some of the diverse life situations, experiences, emotional states, circumstances and themes which, as consulting readers, we encounter.

Our physical, emotional, vocational, mental and spiritual lives are represented in the 5 Realms. In as much as is possible I've listed each theme under its governing element.

Many of these umbrella themes have their own sub-set of diverse yet related counselling and coaching topics; these lists are not exhaustive.

Like doorways opening to that area of the person's life, many themes are directly identifiable from the forms and features of the hands, while others go beyond hands and cannot be seen in the hands directly, in which case, the features of the hands themselves don't directly correlate, but the themes emerge through dialogue.

Earth Counseling and Coaching Themes

The Physical Realm

Health • Family

Home • Country • Money

The primary areas of human experience which constitute the earth realm are physical health, family dynamics, home, country and money. We also touch on several earth governed emotions in this realm.

Administration and Business

Matters to do with wills, insurances, investments and other practical and administrative issues are themes which regularly arise in readings. While as readers we aren't financial advisors, we are well-advised to steer clients towards taking care of any neglected administrative obligations.

Astute lateral thinkers and problem solvers, those with talent in financial planning and management, who have entrepreneurial orientations, with business savvy and a feel for the flow of money and who may have sudden concepts and springing up of ideas have:

- Minor air lines are clear, straight and do not intersect main earth lines - business acumen, thinks intuitively and out the box
- Upturn in flow of main air lines - a catchment for money
- Long air fingers - clever, shrewd thinker
- Long fire level phalanges - practical, executive and administrative skill
- Tips of fingers square shaped - administrative abilities
- Fire level phalanges long - executive, practical capability

113

Allergy

While earth is the primary governing element of all dis-ease, allergies, where the body's immune system reacts negatively to the allergen, relate to water and air imbalance.

- Lower minor water lines, curved - susceptibility to allergic reactions
- Water shaped hands - sensitivity
- Water skin texture - hyper-responsiveness
- Many fine lines - acute sensitivity

Childhood

Indications of early life challenges, of troubled home atmospheres that are or were disruptive and heavily oppressive or austere show in hands. The hands of those who have had secure and happy childhoods won't have the listed markings, but situations where violence or passive aggression may have played out between the parents, where misunderstandings, emotional and physical abuse and loneliness pervade, are seen in these signs:

- Spikiness, an overall messy look to start of main earth and air lines - strife, oppression, disruption in childhood
- Water line begins extremely spiky - early life emotional strife
- Detachment lines - disassociation
- Very hollow palms - early exile from home
- Low-set thin baby fingers - deficit father function
- Air fingers wide set - alienation

Children

For those clients who ask if they will have children, it is more valuable to enquire into what their emotional charge is around the outcome. Rather than trying to predict the future, it's the exploring of the person's mind-set, hopes, longings and perceptions that adds authenticity to the reading. Picking up the when, gender and number of children in hands would be a psychic perception that might for highly intuitive readers channel through, but some people have numerous 'children lines' yet have no children; the answer is not literally in the lines of the hands. Children lines are:

- Fine lines which cross, ascend or descend from relationship/marriage/affection lines
- Ascending lines - sons
- Descending lines - daughters

Depletion

The amount of fundamental vitality or lack of can be easily identified in a set of hands. We find signs of tiredness, depletion, low libido, weakness of constitution along with diminished power, courage and tenacity in:

- Venus mount flat, flabby, dry, lifeless or even almost hollow - life force very low
- Lines that fall downwards from earth lines - leaked energies, exhaustion
- Pale, soft hands - illness, depression
- Faint lines - sensitivity, weakened life skills, poor resources, tires easily
- Pale hands - weakened energetic field
- Very hollow palms, hands feel thin in the middle - uncomfortable delicacy, fragile constitution

Digestion

In a general sense, the earth element governs food. However, food also sub-categorizes into element governed food types. Grains and staples are earth governed, fruit and vegetables are governed by water, spicy and fast foods by fire and junk foods by air. The condition of people's digestive systems is evidenced in hands. Vulnerable digestion shows up in:

- Islanded earth lines - digestion erratic, reflux, IBS
- Thick and furry earth lines - sluggish digestion, constipation
- Very fine, bitty and delicate earth lines - poor digestive health
- Minor air lines intersect with earth lines - digestive sensitivities
- Bent earth fingers - predisposition to digestive disorders

Divorce

We pick up on themes related to painful disappointments, hurt, breakups, divorce, short-lived affairs and disillusion in love relationships in:

- Branches falling from water lines - disappointment
- Water lines have duplicated sections - double life, duplicity, affairs

Family

Another vast counseling and coaching topic with many possible variations is the relationship between parents and children. Parents often present with the theme of their being unhappy and troubled because of their child's behavior. In these situations, we might explore the possibility that happy parents make happy kids and not the other way around, that the child is oppressed and helpless in the face of their parent's unhappiness.

Common scenarios in family dynamics are adoption, physical and mental disabilities in family members, management of ageing and dying parents and issues to do with pets. The familial situations emerge through dialogue. There are no definitive signs in a set of hands that 'show' adoption. Ties to family might be observed through:

- Earth and air lines joined at their start and remain intertwined along their trajectory - closeness to family, family values are strong
- Lower minor water lines straight, cross earth lines - co-dependency
- Minor earth lines intersect with earth lines - family help in career
- Minor earth begins inside earth - dependence on family, working with family

Father

Psychological consequences of absence of the father function include poor esteem, sexual self-doubt, patterns of abuse in relationships, unconscious scorn and disdain towards men, lack of respect for the father and inability to trust. Deficits, especially in puberty/ adolescence of healthy father functions such as physical and emotional presence, quality time, disciplined guidance, setting of boundaries, protection, provision, and validating the child as being a person in their own right are seen in:

- Air fingers low-set, retract into palms - deficit of emotional and/or physical father function especially in adolescence
- Thin, small air fingers - poor confidence, sexual self-doubt
- Thin bent water fingers - damaged self-esteem
- Radial loops on water fingers - history of severely felt criticism

Food

As an umbrella theme, matters to do with food and eating reach to many associated issues. People's relationship with their body image and their weight is an extremely common counseling and coaching theme. Predisposition to weight gain, or any other food preoccupation that borders on or spills into an eating disorder might be revealed by:

117

- Very thin fingers - fastidious, abstemious, frugal
- Full, plump water level phalanges - security sought in material world
- Full, plump base of water fingers - loves food, given to excess
- Grilles on basal phalanges, especially of water fingers - desire vs restriction
- Lower minor water lines straight - obsessive, addictive trends

Generosity

The act of giving so as to uplift, enlighten and relieve others plays out in philanthropy and in simple day-to-day material, spiritual and emotional generosity. Those who seeks to promote the welfare of others, whether through donating money or giving of time, have these indications in their hands:

- Earth lines curved, sweep wide - generosity
- Water lines extend from ulnar to radial edge - "Humanitarian lines"
- Healing stigmata - compassion
- Thick fingers - innate sense of abundance
- Earth shaped hands - kindness
- Fingers, outward leaning, wide-open - open-heartedness

Health

At the base of the 5 Realm model is that which is fundamental to all facets of our well-being, our health. Predisposition to and manifestation of many ailments are evidenced in our palms. Scientific medical research into the prognostic value of identifying potential and manifest disease in hands is a growing field. Researchers claim that conditions such as Alzheimer's, schizophrenia, personality disorders, autism, cancers and leukemia, reproductive disorders, respiratory and cardio-vascular disorders, congenital and acquired heart disease, Down's and other syndromes, diabetes, endocrine imbalances and digestive disorders can be medically diagnosed from skin ridge patterns, linear formations and nails. Different disease manifestations each have their own central element.

Earth -   skeletal and digestive systems, teeth, nails
Water -   urinary and reproductive systems, lymph, skin, emotional imbalance
Fire -   endocrine, vascular, metabolism, muscular system
Air –   nervous system, respiratory system, brain
Aether - mental illness, phobias, psychopathy

Earth is the primary governor of the realm of physical health, but in that disease is not just in the body, it's from this basis of materiality that health conditions further sub-categorize. Imbalances are sourced within the multi-dimensional strata of all the realms. In conversation with chirology, we discuss physical, emotional, mental and spiritual wellness.

Hand readers aren't authorized to diagnose, but we do pick up relatively minor or even more serious ailments. If through the hand feature we intuitively and confidently sense that the person's health issue is relatively minor, perhaps a comforting comment, such as "you are wounded, but you are not diseased" is helpful. A generalized mention, such as "How is your lower back?" or "Your digestive tract is showing as a sensitive area" is appropriate. These are examples of ethical entrées and invitations to the person to share about any health struggles they may experience. If the person's biochemistry is clearly imbalanced and we are alerted to a more serious health concern, we gently refer to a doctor. When they share of a diagnosed condition, we support them in finding ways to support themselves, such as with integrative healing therapies, nutrition, remedies and supplements.

Home Life

Is the person rooted in traditional values? Do they have deep attachments to family and strive for their kin? Do they love their country of origin and have a strong sense of national or ethnic group identity? Is security and the sense of belonging of paramount importance? Do they love their home? The orientation towards continuity, sustenance and preservation of familial, cultural and social groups is seen in:

- Earth lines long, cling tightly to base of Venus mounts - traditional values, fond attachment to hearth and home
- Earth and air lines which joined at their start and only separate further along their trajectory - family allegiance, respect for parents
- Earth shaped hands - traditional values

Honesty

"Love bounces, but trust breaks."   *Lazaris*

Earth governed traits and themes that relate to honesty, loyalty, integrity, trustworthiness and their opposites of betrayal, deception and duplicity regularly arise in chirology readings. Often, a person who has little internal reference for lies and deception has had their trust broken; they are suffering greatly. Conversely, another situation arises where, to their utmost guilt and dismay, a person who is essentially honest lands in a position that requires duplicity, where they are out of integrity with their own innate values. Signs that might take us into this topic include:

- Earth shaped hands - can add to trustworthiness
- Broad base of hands - reliability
- Arches - commitment, conservative values, what you see is what you get
- Water lines short, straight - bearer doesn't trust easily

- Earth (Venus) mount crease - loyalty, honesty, deception, duplicity, morality issues, susceptibility to betrayal and betraying
- Serious intent loops - sobriety, high principles
- Water lines duplicated - double life
- Air fingers bent - lies, untrustworthiness

Humiliation

"When pride comes, then comes disgrace,
but with humility comes wisdom." Proverbs 11:2

Humiliation, encountered by most at some stage in life, is an agonizing emotion. The psychologically distressing effects of humiliation's shame, embarrassment, loss of dignity and anger can be so severely crippling that it is experienced as intensely as physical pain. For some people, the mental distress caused by the utter mortification of one or many humiliating incidents will exacerbate anxiety and depression to the extent that the sufferer may withdraw, isolate, and abandon any inspired directive. The heart-shrivelling resentment at having been humiliated might have been carried for years. When clients present with the feelings of past and/or current humiliation, how might we support them?

Unpacking resentments and exploring self and other forgiveness are important first ports of call. Then to consider looking at humiliation through the lens of the worthy virtue of humility. Defined as the quality of being humble, of having a modest view of one's importance, the Latin root of 'humiliation' is 'humus', which translates as 'earth' or 'dirt'. Humus is that which breaks down, which decomposes and nourishes the earth so as to facilitate a resilient regrowth from the soil.

Through this lens, we might consider encouraging and supporting the client to drop deep, down into the crushing sensation of disintegration, to where the layer of humus is most fertile. Feeling it

121

is healing it; within the crisis is opportunity. The experience of humiliation can lead to the emergence of humility, new insights, improved self-worth and increased dignity.

- Red knuckles - may be a history of being humiliated
- Red hands - emotional strain, humiliation
- Water finger thin, bent inwards to earth - person feels 'done in', victimized

Inheritance

The ramifications and consequences of all aspects to do with inheritance is a fairly common theme. Markings which open to the likelihood in the person's life of manifested or potential inheritances include:

- A single deep line on Sun mount of passive hand - inheritance, financial support, safety net
- Minor earth lines doubled - two sources of income

Inner Child

For those of us who carry the lingering effects of unresolved childhood wounds, inner child work is a powerfully integrative process. As adults, our inner child is an alive part of ourselves which reactively trips us up in triggering situations.

For many people, the helpful process of communing with, befriending and healing the wounded inner child is a necessary part of becoming a well-integrated adult.

The process begins with acknowledgement that the inner child's emotions are causing dysfunction in adulthood. For clients who are open to exploring their relationship with their inner child, one suggested way to begin to meet the inner child's needs is to write them letters in which the situations where emotional support, recognition, praise and other unmet needs are compassionately recalled and acknowledged.

Another powerful process is inner dialogue. In the metaphysical realm of meditative stillness, we address our inner child as a person. In listening for and receiving impressions of vulnerabilities, hurts, fears and anxieties, for rejection, abandonment and insecurity and for anger, guilt and shame, authentic feelings are identified and validated. The internal dialogue facilitates a re-parenting. With questions like "How do you feel?" and "What do you need from me?" we envisage and convey parental qualities of love, nurturing and protection.

When using this process with a client, they might for example report sensing, seeing and experiencing their inner child as a feral entity who is trapped, spitting, hissing and cornered. That this vision appears so clearly affords an opportunity; here this terrified sub-personality can be determinedly held and soothed until they feel calm. In offering full acceptance to the exiled inner child, the image positively transforms. A naturally playful and magical inner child who looks at life through eyes of wonder soon emerges. This fascinatingly transformative practice can be done in minutes and is a very helpful way to deepen into self-love.

Kindness

Kind hands are easy to spot. An energy exudes from these hands that is unmistakable. Themes that may arise when counseling a kind person are their tendency to over-give, the likelihood of naively attracting people into their lives who use and abuse them and the importance of boundaries.

- Earth shaped hands - tolerance, kindness
- Arches - kindness, compassion
- Wide sweep of earth lines - charitable, generosity with money

- Water lines straight, reach radial edge - humanitarian, social activism, extended emotional range
- Water lines forked - tolerance for other's orientations and proclivities
- Mounts full and fleshy - nurturing
- Empathy loops - empathic qualities, compassion for others
- Thumbs wide set - generosity of spirit
- Thumbs clubbed - humility, gentleness, kindness, sweetness of nature

Lower Back

Skeletally, the base of our spines is perhaps our most likely area of weakness. Clients with potential or manifested lower back inflammation could have:

- Messy or islanded base of earth and start of minor earth lines – 1st and 2nd chakra vulnerability

Money

The theme of money is an umbrella with many facets; this is a burning issue for many. In the context of the 5 Realm model, we offer at least some mention of financial and administrative matters; clients often want to discuss their struggles or successes with wealth accumulation. Conversations in the realm of finances include practical circumstances, property or other investments, inheritance, lack of money, sense of deservability, the interplay of self-worth and self-esteem with the bank balance or lack of, what might constitute enough money, wills, insurance policies and any other administrative matters.

Many clients ask about whether they will be lucky with money, but perhaps the saying "the harder you work, the luckier you will be" might apply. Indicators in hands of money related matters are:

- Earth lines curve tight to cramp Venus mounts - short arms, long pockets
- Fingers held tightly together - reduced generosity
- Nails that grow inwards towards the palms - materialistic tendencies
- Fingers all curve inwards towards earth fingers - acquisitiveness
- Fleshy basal phalanges - love of luxury
- Rings on earth fingers - person needs security
- Waisted basal phalanges, light seen when fingers are held together - money leaks away
- Bendy back thumbs - person likes to spend
- Stars on Sun mounts - warmth, attracts wealth
- Peacock's eyes on fire fingers - luck
- Air lines curve upwards, pull to Mercury at their ends - a catchment for money, business acumen
- Single vertical minor fire lines under fire fingers - attracts wealth

Mother

There are signs in hands of a difficult mother relationship and of deficient maternal nurturing and support. The mother may have been physically absent, narcissistic, compulsive or otherwise disordered or substance addicted.

In hands of those who have complex mother relationships, or who were maternally abandoned, separated from and uncared for we find:

- Cramp lines - intense psychical attachment and sensitization to mother's physical and emotional experience
- Lower minor water lines run into Venus mounts - addictive/obsessive traits in lineage, co-dependency
- Falling lines from main water lines - emotional hurt and pain

Moving House - Emigration - Immigration

The likelihood in a person's life of their moving house or moving away from their country of origin have reliable associated palmar markings:

- Earth lines send branches to Moon, Neptune or Pluto mounts - geographical moves
- Travel lines - restlessness, wanting change

Reproductive Organs

Fertility is a theme that arises for both men and women, along with other related reproductive system conditions, such as low libido, impotence, endometriosis, irregular periods and prostate, ovarian and uterine health. Signs of vulnerability are:

- Top rascettes ('bracelet' lines on wrists) break and lift towards palms - long believed to aspect the health of reproductive organs
- The base of the earth and minor earth lines are islanded, spiky and messy - 2nd chakra vulnerability

Resentment

The emotion of resentment is often buried; thus it is earth governed. Resentment is defined as bitter indignation at having been treated unfairly. Clients who habitually revisit negative thoughts of wrongs done to them need supportive guidance as to how to break free from holding onto the past. Resentments are bondages; as the saying goes, a negative thought about another person is like eating poison and then expecting that person to die.

Forgiveness, prayers for the well-being of those people we resent, self-compassion and letting go are all key to healing. Additionally, a very empowering and enlightening practice for those who are willing to live without resentments, who want to break this difficult pattern, is to 'download' a resentment journal.

In a notebook, we assign the header "I resent myself for..." to a few pages; these are for listing memories of where we have let ourselves down. This is a way of taking responsibility for our role in the situations.

Childhood rejection and criticism and the resulting insecurity make us prone to harboring resentments, so we continue with "I resent my mother for ... ", "I resent my father for ... " We then allocate pages for everyone in life who has offended; the possibilities include siblings, children, friends, colleagues, bosses, staff, the government, religious leaders and even God. Over a period of several months, each time a memory of a perceived wrong doing surfaces, no matter how old, slight or silly, to write it down. Depending upon the extent of injustice, we may be able to bring playfulness to the process. In casting a light of awareness, many resentments are often quite funny to own up to; the charge quickly dissolves. Look for:

- Arches - buried emotions
- Hard hands with stiff fingers - intractable mind-sets
- Fingers and/or nails curve towards palms - rigidity, bitterness

Responsibility

"Responsibility and freedom go together.
If you don't want to take responsibility,
you can't have freedom either.
The two come together or they go together.
If you shun responsibility,
you have to accept slavery in some way or other." Osho

Those who as a life theme bear significant responsibility, who are hard-working and accountable are very likely to have:

- Earth shaped hands - steadiness of purpose

127

- Minor earth lines well formed, run over Saturn mounts into base of earth fingers - responsibility as a life lesson
- Arches - dutifulness, adherence to tasks
- Serious intent loops - work ethic, conscientiousness, or the opposite, procrastination
- Long straight earth fingers - sobriety of thought

Self-worth

Feeling less-than is a function of the negative ego and is as egotistic as feeling better than others. The theme of how to up-level and sustain an internal sense of being good enough pertains to almost everyone. Countless people share of how easily they default from any feelings of positive self-regard to feeling bad, wrong and unworthy of love. Or worse, they have an entrenched and continual anxieties about their credibility and a very poor opinion of themselves. In readings, the conversation about crisis of confidence and the painful consequences of low self-worth might begin through observation of:

- Passive hand messy, active hand clear - true feelings hidden by projected persona
- Water fingers bent - self-criticism, judgment, person feels inadequate or 'done in'
- Water fingers short - low self-esteem
- Short low set air fingers - feel unsupported
- Thumbs held close to hands - poor confidence
- High set thumbs - little sense of personal power
- Thumb tips bend inward – giving up/in, unhappiness, fearfulness
- Radial loops on water fingers - crushed from criticism in childhood
- Rings on water fingers - need for more respect and authority
- Upper minor water lines - not good enough, exacting standards

Tremors

Tremoring hands have many possible root causes; stress or shock, or too much caffeine, or a sudden drop in blood pressure, or the gradual weakening of the nervous system due to aging. CPTSD, PTSD and chronic anxiety also cause tremoring. More severe forms of tremors in hands occur with mercury poisoning, alcohol abuse and withdrawal and as a side effect of many toxic drugs. Tremoring is also symptomatic with thyroid, liver, kidneys, multiple sclerosis, Parkinson's and other lesser-known degenerative syndromes.

Some people suffer constant shakiness without any definable cause; in this case the involuntary movements of their hands is likely caused by a fairly common and benign neurological condition known as the essential, familial or idiopathic tremor, the cause of which is unknown.

More Earth Themes

Abortion	Doing things in their rightful order
Administrative matters	
Adoption	Eating Disorders
Aging	Emigration
Allergy	Family Dynamics
Animals	Father
Boundaries	Generosity
Business Acumen	Health
Childhood	Home life
Children	Honesty (with self and others)
Country	House moves
Depletion	Humiliation and humility
Deservability	Immigration
Diagnostics	Inheritance
Digestion	Inner child
Disability	Kindness
Disasters	Lower back
Divorce	Money

Mother
Parenting
Procrastination
Resentment
Resistance
Responsibility
Self-doubt

Self-esteem/self-worth
Shame fortress
Socioeconomic status
Step-parents
Teens
Tremors

Water Counseling and Coaching Themes

The Emotional Realm

Intimacy • Sexuality

Relationships • Friendships

Emotional Wellness

Social Life • Community Service

In counseling and coaching with chirology, the realm of water encompasses these primary areas of human experience: the interplays of relationships and friendships, intimacy and sexuality, social life, community service, water governed emotions and overall emotional wellness.

Co-Dependency

Co-dependency is a symptom of Self-Love Deficit Disorder (SLDD). The dis-ease of co-dependency stems from early life emotional neglect which disables the ability to self-love. Co-dependent people try to fill painful emptiness through reliance on outward-focused behaviors, on anything external that might provide temporary relief or validation. In that co-dependent people want someone or something external to rescue them from themselves, the emotional and behavioral condition results in a high level of susceptibility to forming relationships that are destructive and abusive.

Typically, co-dependency plays out in love addiction, sex addiction, substance addiction and becoming engulfed and enmeshed in relationships with narcissists. Through the lens of "if I keep you happy you will love and protect me" the compliant codependent will do anything to avoid abandonment. They have no boundaries; they hand over their rights, enable other's destructive behaviors, do as others want and try to avoid criticism by excessively worrying about what others think of them. An exaggerated sense of responsibility for the actions of others, where they avoid their own needs and instead obsessively try to control, help or fix others, is another sign.

In active co-dependency, sufferers live in a vibrational field of high drama; they are hyper-vigilant, yet cannot take responsibility and are unwilling and unable to face the true source of their problems. They are at odds with life, blame others, feel taken advantage of and see themselves as victims of the many seemingly insolvable problems they are typically entangled in.

Co-dependents commonly, but not invariably, grow up with alcoholic or other substance addicted parent(s). The healing of co-dependency requires cultivating conscious, authentic and sustained self-love and self-acceptance. Resources to help co-dependents to heal include the 12 Step Program of Co-dependents Anonymous, counseling and online support forums. Signs of co-dependency in hands include:

- Lower minor water lines cross into Venus mounts - co-dependency, torrents of obsessive thinking
- Earth and fire fingers held tightly together - insecurity

Depression

Depression is a water governed feeling. We drown in its depths, in an implosion of energy that perhaps keeps a lid on anger. For reasons sourced in lineage, chemistry, circumstances and attitudes, a barrage of negative, destructive thoughts and emotions pervade the psyche. There are several features in hands that aspect depressive tendencies. Markings that might open the conversation with clients who clearly are struggling include:

- Moist hands - feelings running high
- Air lines slope steeply to end in Moon mounts - thinking is deeply bound up with feeling
- Falling lines from earth lines - leakage of energy, weakened resources
- Falling lines from water lines - disappointment, hurts, upsets
- Very long earth fingers - solemnity could turn pessimistic
- Earth fingers bend to fire fingers - introspection, self-criticism, happiness made guilty by duty
- Upper minor water lines - 'divine discontent' with exacting, never good enough idealism
- Upper minor water lines, striated - disillusion, despair
- Inward-bending thumbs - unbearable trauma, anxiety, depression
- A 'flare' of many fine lines covering the plain of Mars - unhappiness with a current life situation
- Moon mounts overly large - moodiness, emotionalism
- Double loop dermatoglyphics on Moon mounts - turbulent emotions, 'in the wishy washy'

Emotional Balance

As readers we endeavour to learn what we can of the range of human emotion. In readings, our enquiry reveals how the client is generally feeling. Are they clinically depressed or do they have a diagnosis such as bi-polar? Are they coping emotionally? Are they high on the neuroticism scale? Do they experience intense mood fluctuations and how stable are they?

- Very flexible hands - add more water to psyche
- Thin fingers - life's demands are hard
- Puffy mounts - emotional responses
- Faint and fading lines - sensitivity and low energy
- Small thumbs - childlike traits
- Simian lines - alternates between emotional extremes

Empaths

Empaths take the natural quality of empathy for others to another level; they are highly sensitive people who are so fine-tuned, psychically open and connected to unseen subtle realms that their subjective experience is of being incessantly inundated, invaded or even assaulted by other people's pain, which is felt as their own. Empaths are creatively, artistically and intuitively gifted but their constant picking up on and absorbing impressions of positive and negative vibrational nuance is exhausting and is often felt as a curse rather than a blessing.

Support for empaths involves identification and validation of their experience. As readers we don't tell them they are "too sensitive" but instead offer embrace, compassion and education about what it means to be an empath, and how to manage their interface with living.

One telling characteristic of an empath is their instantaneous awareness of other's energy. Other signs are social anxiety, finding crowds and excessive noise unbearable and susceptibility to erratic fluctuations in both mood and behavior. They mostly have an 'inward' default of introversion, but can swing to peaky, over-aroused excitable and energetically outward-driven interludes. Stimulants cause extremely adverse effects. In their attempts to self-medicate, they may battle with eating and other addictions.

To sustain emotional balance and manage feelings of being exhausted and drained, empaths need to set parameters for what does and does not work and to cognitively use tools and techniques to put protective measures into place. Social media offers many support groups where empaths are encouraged to practice tenderness towards themselves and to establish organized routines where they can disentangle from overwhelming stimulus. Staying grounded in the daily life of an empath requires setting boundaries, periodic retreat to a quiet, alone space and immersion in creative endeavor.

Empaths are like moths to a flame to narcissists and often attach co-dependently; the narcissist's pain attracts the empaths impulse to comfort and heal.

- Water shaped hands - vulnerability, easily drained
- Faint lines - need peace and quiet
- Skin moist, soft - takes things personally, impressionable
- Upper minor water lines - striated - emotional hypersensitivity, easily hurt
- Lines excessive, fine - wired nervous systems, Highly Sensitive People (HSP's), acute sensitivity
- Droplets on fingers - sensitivity to suffering

Forgiveness

The theme of forgiveness of others as well as self-forgiveness are significant topics which very often feature in the context of a hand reading experience.

One way to support clients who struggle with the theme of forgiveness is to explore the possibility of compassionately forgiving the "why". In deepening into an understanding of the formative influences of the perpetrator, we open to forgiving the why and immediately feel kinder. At the same time, we are not expected to forgive the often unforgiveable "what".

When presented with the possibility of embracing the polarity of both forgiving and not forgiving, an expanded sense of letting what is be there will arise. We forgive the why, but not the what; we allow the feelings to be there and make peace with what happened.

Grief

While grief can often be seen in the hands, experienced readers will readily feel the person's aura of sadness even without looking at their hands. Grief counseling is a specialized field and referral to a professional might be indicated, nevertheless we are well-advised to at least learn some basic guidelines about the stages of grief and the tasks of mourning.

We acknowledge suffering by affirming the client's loss of person or animal and how difficult it is. It's helpful to understand that people grieve differently. Some clients are openly devastated and overwhelmed; exhausting emotions and physical symptoms render them incapable of functioning; with these clients we can sensitively ask how they are coping. Others grieve mentally and privately and are unwilling or unable to show feelings; here we don't push them to share.

Guilt often accompanies grief; those whose style of grieving is thoughtful, internal and reserved might feel guilty, perhaps for not feeling sad enough, or for appearing cold and not feeling or behaving in ways that they think others expect from them. Commonly, guilt is felt around what was or was not done while their loved one was alive.

When grief is a primary theme in a chirology reading, we make sure to distinguish grief from trauma. Those who are suffering traumatic grief, such as with miscarriages, violent deaths and suicide where both trauma and bereavement coincide, may struggle to get an image out of their head, or experience flashbacks. To open the way for grief, the extent of the trauma needs to be recognized and attended to.

Bereavement counselors are taught that death ends life, but not necessarily the relationship. For the bereaved, adjusting to life and moving on without the person or pet is made easier when rather than relinquishing their bond, a communion of a different kind takes the place of physical presence. There are recommendations we might offer that will help the bereaved to cultivate an ongoing sense of heart-felt connection to the person or pet that has passed. Regular sharing of memories, commemorative rituals like lighting candles or re-visiting photos and videos, getting a symbolic tattoo, traveling to the places that the departed person loved or wanted to visit, meeting with spiritual readers who channel from beyond the veil, visiting their grave and planting a tree in memory of the person are some suggestions. We might suggest that our client considers joining a grief support group where they meet with and are supported by grief survivors who are further along in their grieving process.

Indications in hands of the person being in a torrent of emotional pain, sorrow and grief include:

- Pale hands - shock, grief
- Water lines are broken, overlapped, damaged - trauma
- Falling lines from water lines - despair, sadness
- Cold clammy hands - emotional trauma

Idealism

Perfectionism is unattainable, its pursuit is doomed to fail, and worse, it fosters the voice of the punitive inner critic. Idealism is the antithesis of true creativity; it's exacting standards cannot be met. Signs in hands of wanting it perfect are:

- Upper minor water lines - exacting standards, own worst critic, nothing is ever good enough
- Water shaped hands - perfectionism, idealism
- Water lines run into water fingers - increased idealism
- Water fingers pointed - hyper-critical, exacting, fastidiousness
- Big hands, disproportionate to body size - fussiness, exacting standards

Insecurity

Plaguing feelings of insecurity have their source in ancestral persecution, trauma, childhood formative influences and physical, financial, educational and vocational circumstances, but are also interwoven with difficulty in taking responsibility and giving away of power. No amount of external approval or validation heals insecurity; self-love is the elixir. In hands, feelings of being unsafe show up in:

- Rings on all digits - hides behind display, insecurity
- Earth fingers bend to fire - instability, introversion, insecurity
- Short water fingers - low self-esteem
- Radial loops on water fingers - chameleon, adapts to fit in
- Fingers held closely together - shyness, apprehension, inhibition
- Air fingers short, low set - timidity, poor confidence
- Upper minor water lines - not good enough
- Thumbs held - doubts, fears, anxiety
- Thumb tips bend inwards - un-confidence, reduced self-determination

Manipulation

Like two sides of the same coin, features in hands that signal a tendency in a person to be manipulative also show the flip side; that the person might be easily manipulated. Clients often seek support for challenging work and relationship situations, where they feel like a human marshmallow, used, overworked but under-employed and undervalued. Other clients come across as being manipulative; they are passive aggressive, shift blame, avoid truthfulness, beg for help but remain wilful and controlling. Signs in hands of traits related to manipulation are:

- Water hand shape - gets what wants, easily influenced
- Water skin texture - tenacity of purpose, malleability
- Soft flexible hands - manipulative traits, easily influenced
- Pale skin - manipulation through weakness, payoffs
- Straight water line with upper minor water line - exacting criteria, impossible to please
- Water fingers wide set - bossy, controlling nature
- Air fingers bent - distorted communications
- Thumbs, large tips - wilfulness
- Thumbs, flexible, bendy - manipulation, easily influenced,
- Thumbs spoke shaved - opportunism, shrewdness
- Nails grow inwards - self-serving, self-centred
- Thumbs bend inwards - fear, control through weakness
- Fingers leaning to radial side - dependency
- Double loop dermatoglyphics - vacillation
- Attachment lines - neediness, insecurity

Narcissistic Abuse

A critical conversation for many clients is the identification and validation of their soul-shattering annihilation at the hands of a true narcissist. Unfortunately, many doctors and therapists don't comprehend or take cognizance of the dire consequences of narcissistic abuse in their patient's lives. For those who haven't experienced narcissistic abuse, the effects are almost unfathomable. This is a vitally important counseling and coaching theme that all therapists should know about so as to validate their client's situation.

In conversation, we find a spectrum of possibilities; whether the narcissists in their lives are parents, partners or children, some clients are informed of what they are dealing with, while others are so co-dependently enmeshed that they are unable to hear or integrate the possibility that they are being abused. This takes gentle navigation; for them, the start of disentangling and healing is all in the timing and has yet to begin.

There are specific red flags that identify whether a client is entangled in a narcissistically abusive relationship. These include the sense of their perpetually walking on eggshells around the person, feelings of increasing worthlessness, along with obsessional psychic, mental and emotional focus on their narcissistic partner/parent/child. The relationship is infused with constant dramas; nothing is ever right enough. Arguments are incessant and provoked over the slightest, mostly irrational issues. The arguing may or may not be physically abusive, but will include being battered with a barrage of word salad, of being talked at, with non-sensical conversations from hell where nothing is ever properly discussed. An increasing sense of isolation is another red flag; narcissists often discourage or even prohibit friendships, or will close ranks and triangulate with a third person, thereby further isolating their victim.

Like a Jekyll and Hyde, narcissists shape shift; victims endure cycles of idealization and love bombing, where it goes from you are their all and everything to sudden projection of their toxic shame. In this part of the cycle, victims endure devaluating put downs and blaming criticisms, angry outbursts, cruel contempt, emotional withdrawal and cold silent treatment. Their need for power and control and their pleasure in provoking and emotionally breaking their victim is clearly evidenced in a momentary smile of contemptuous delight known as the 'narcissistic smirk'. Once their emotional invalidation evokes sufficient distress and drama, the narcissist's need for narcissistic supply is met and they swing back to being sweet, charming and seemingly remorseful.

Throughout the cycles, the distorting and eroding technique of gaslighting prevails. Gaslighting is subtle psychological manipulation that is used to make a person question their perception of reality. Even in the face of clear evidence, gaslighters lie about things that are true. Tactics include claiming loss of memory, denial that situations even happened, speaking badly of their victim's loved ones, projection of their negative traits, and provoking. Once they have a rise of anger or emotion, they displace blame and make the the person into the problem. By hearing that they are negative, or too sensitive, the person is gaslit to believe that their sense of reality is inaccurate, that they are at fault, are the abuser, or even that the abuse never happened. Victims become trauma bonded in a confusion of pain, love and bio-chemical peptide addiction to melodramas; these negative emotional and physical states further enmesh them in the destructive relationship.

In cases where there is physical threat, establishing physical safety is first priority. Going no contact is ultimately the best option, but where this is impossible, 'going grey rock' is a way to begin to disentangle. Like water off a duck's back, going grey rock means not getting hooked; instead meeting the narcissist with boring, monotonous responses. Narcissists cannot be without drama; when met with grey rock they lose interest and will soon look for new supply.

There is commonality between co-dependency and narcissism; they are two sides of the same coin. Narcissists and co-dependents alike seek validation from others, regulate their self-esteem through others and are not capable of being the source of self-love to themselves. Both exhibit controlling behaviors and are hyper-vigilant. Both have the same painful emptiness and both are deeply wounded.

Healing from narcissistic abuse begins by encouraging victims to take responsibility, to mourn appropriately for what is lost, to build safe relationships and to accept that the narcissist entered their life as a messenger to alert them to their own unhealed wounds.

Narcissistic Personality Disorder (NPD)

The staggering extent of the epidemic of NPD is evidenced in the ocean of shared information that is readily available on social media. Narcissism plays out in several guises; from the overt, obviously self-absorbed grandiose narcissist, to the more insidious covert or vulnerable narcissist, who is the consummate actor and almost impossible to categorize or diagnose.

Behaviorally, narcissists exhibit specific, consistent and recognizable traits. As readers, we might intuitively sense that something is very awry with a narcissistic client. In conversation with a person who we suspect rates high on the narcissistic spectrum, we might observe that they seem humble, but are presenting an unnecessarily charming and manipulative false self. This person vehemently monitors how we perceive them, believes that they are the victim and blames their emotional pain on anything other than themselves.

Like sociopaths and psychopaths, they are void of empathy and so deeply wounded and filled with self-loathing that they cannot love. Narcissists are terminally co-dependent and are unable to heal; they are incapable of accountability and highly unlikely to successfully take responsibility or commit to self-reflection. Types and degrees of narcissism present on too a broad a spectrum for us to be able to definitively diagnose or verify the disorder though hand features; the counseling and coaching theme emerges through intuitive insight and conversation.

Relationships

Matters to do with relationships are the single biggest topic in all consultations, (with the realm of work/life purpose being the second most common theme). Whether with ourselves, partners, children, friends, siblings, parents, bosses or anyone else, this essential water governed theme is of an enormously broad spectrum; it embraces everything to do with how we relate. Difficulty with making friends and loneliness also fall under this umbrella.

It is a myth that the number of relationships, marriages, separations and divorces a person will have can be seen in their palms. A mention that couples counseling is a specialized field; when a couple asks for help to heal their relationship, consider referral to Imago therapists or other couples specialists.

Our styles of interactivity with our fellow people and animals are to a certain extent reflected in almost all hand features, but some hand features that refer us directly to relationship issues are:

- Main water lines - form and flow represent styles of relating
- Relationship (affection) lines - levels reveal preferred values e.g. security, emotional support, friendship, sex, companionship
- Water lines with falling lines - disappointment, grief, loss
- Water lines repeatedly print with hollow white splotch - shock, crisis

Self-pity

"Self-pity is our worst enemy and if we yield to it, we can never do anything wise in this world."   Helen Keller

Sometimes a gloomy client who is extremely absorbed in their troubles and who comes across as being immersed in self-pity will respond well if we honestly and directly address the issue by stating: "you are stuck in self-pity." As a reader, this begs delicate navigation; intuition will guide as to whether or not the client is ready and willing to confront this uncomfortable truth.

If it feels right to 'go' there, we can offer clients an objective exploration into why people 'do' self-pity, a look at the various types of self-pity, and enquire as to where they might identify their personal 'brand' of self pity. This then becomes an interesting topic and an entrée into self-awareness and growth.

Habituated self-pity is toxic and self-destructive. The pre-occupation is manipulative; through righteousness and weakness we try to elicit some sort of payoff or guarantee, but instead, self-pity sustains a sense of separateness. In self-pity, we are unconsciously looking to be rescued and are avoidant of taking responsibility for our present reality.

There are seven readily identifiable types of self-pity. Victims wallow in their sorry tales and have insatiable cravings for others' sympathy; the world is against them, nothing is ever enough. Martyrs want to suffer, everything is hopeless and they are the only people who have to endure such hardship. A third way that self-pity plays out is in ceaseless worry and struggle; the attempt to control life overrules any capacity for trusting that existence takes care. Silent competitors measure themselves against others' apparent advantages; you have a beautiful house and family and I don't, therefore "poor me." Blamers hold everyone except themselves accountable for their woes in life. Ego-pamperers are high on the narcissistic spectrum; their needs, no matter how small or random, must come before anyone else's. A seventh expression of self-pity is the savior, the person who goes around doing so much for others, but are themselves hard-done by and full of complaints about how much they do for everyone else yet no one cares enough about them.

As readers, we take an empathic stance; everyone, but especially those who are more melancholy in temperament, has bouts of feeling sorry for themselves; it's a coping mechanism born from genuine suffering, that to some extent brings temporary comfort. Clients ought not to feel judged, but instead be encouraged to see themselves through a nurturing and compassionate lens. Shifting out of a self-pitied mind-set is a process of identifying the voice of the negative ego. This is the part of our psyche that always finds reason to be unhappy. In recognizing the limitations of being governed by unconscious unresolved pain and fear and by harnessing the voice of the negative ego, we begin to deepen into our self-esteem and personal power.

Sexuality

This counseling and coaching theme is broad-reaching, its many facets are beyond the scope of this book, but important is that readers ought not be afraid to open into conversation about intimacy. It is often very relieving for clients to share about their libido, sexual orientation, gender identity, sex and porn addiction, overt or subtle forms of sexual molestation and abuse, too early exposure to sex, impotency, vaginismus and any other variables of this theme. Sexuality is a challenging area for the majority of people. We see indications of people's sexuality in:

- Earth shape - sexually conventional
- Water shape - romance before intimacy
- Fire shape - experiential, longer to commit
- Air shape - visual, friendship important
- Thin soft hands - not so interested in sex, dislike of physical or emotional exertion
- Short straight water lines - passion, but inhibited emotion
- Very hard hands - strength, potency, lack of tenderness
- High set thumbs - repressed sexuality
- Soft big thick hands - sensual but lazy
- Firm hands - energy, sexual potency
- Thick fingers - overabundant desire nature, greed
- Lower minor water line, straight - wants peak experience, strong charge around sex
- Venus mounts flat - no libido, impotence
- Venus mounts full - ardent libido, given to excess, appetite, virility
- Long air fingers - charm, seductiveness, sexiness
- Whorls on air fingers - unorthodox sexual tastes
- Droplets on fingertips - sensuality

Shame

"Shame is a soul eating emotion."   Carl Jung

While guilt says I am sorry I did wrong, I made a mistake, shame says I am wrong, I am a mistake. Deep shame is the rejected part of ourselves that we deem most unlovable; like a defensive, subjectively protective fortress, shame is hidden self-loathing that prevents intimacy and keeps us feeling separate. The emotion of shame is bio-chemically addictive, the feeling releases chemistry into the system. Shame is a self-focused, negative and very toxic emotion; in secrecy, silence and self-judgment, shame grows exponentially.

In conversation, when working with this theme, it is helpful to clarify for clients that people who don't experience shame have no capacity for compassion. There is a way to dismantle the shame-based contracts which keep us locked into mediocre or destructive patterns and behaviors. To reset the condition of our sense of worth, we give shame compassion for human innocence, and the emotion cannot survive. The antidote to shame is empathy.

Awareness in clients of their shame-based responses, that they suffer with the trauma-based, acutely lonely core wound of shame, is a regular counseling and coaching theme in all therapy practices. The theme of shame as evidenced in hands might arise through the observation of:

- Bent water fingers - victim mentality, life has done this to me
- Short water fingers - not good enough, damaged self-esteem
- Small thumbs - reduced coping skills

Social Conscience

Being part of an interrelated community of people is integral to emotional and spiritual wellness; in readings this theme is always worthy of mention and enquiry. We touch on whether the person isolates or actively participates in society and in which ways. We affirm a client's motivation to help others through observing:

- Earth lines sweep wide to middle of hands - generosity of spirit, charity
- Water lines, run across to end on radial edge - 'humanitarian' lines, devotion to just causes

More Water Themes

Abandonment
Activism
Boundaries
Co-dependency
Depression
Disappointment
Divorce
Emotional Balance
Emotionally exhausting to self and others
Empathy
Entitlement, feeling hard done by, that you have a right to have it better
Forgiveness
Friendships
Gratitude
Grief
Highly Sensitive People (HSP's)
Loneliness
Manipulations
Marriage
Martyrhood
Narcissism
Narcissistic abuse

Need to step back from emotional involvements
Others demand that you give more than you have
Parentified children
Pay-offs
Perseverance
Pets
Relationships
Righteousness
Safety
Self-pity
Sexual identity - lesbian, queer, bisexual, transgender
Sexuality
Shame
Shyness
Social conscience – charity – community
Striving for purity
The more I give, the less I get – taken for granted
Trauma bonding
Victim

Fire Counseling and Coaching Themes

The Vocational Realm

Life Purpose • Creativity

Vocation • Vitality

In counseling and coaching with chirology, the realm of fire encompasses these primary areas of human experience: life purpose, career and vocational life, creativity (and the opposite, that of self-sabotaging and destructive patterns), fundamental vitality and joie de vivre, and matters to do with fire governed emotions.

Ambition

Motivation towards success might be in the physical, financial, academic, spiritual or other areas of development. To feel into the likelihood of a competitive streak or the desire in a person for achievement of influence, status and accomplishment, we look for:

- Ambition lines - aspirations to betterment
- Large Jupiter mounts - leadership, outreach
- Long straight water fingers - natural authority
- Serious intent loops - work ethic
- Charisma loops - leadership
- Firm fire shaped hands with fire skin texture - energy
- Long straight thumbs - firm will
- Large fire (tip) phalanges of thumbs - innovative, versatile
- Minor earth line runs towards Jupiter mount - ambition
- Stars on Jupiter and Sun mounts - luck, sudden breaks
- Thumbs held wide - confidence, determination

149

Anger and Rage

In essence the emotion of anger is healthy; it protects boundaries and brings energy and drive to make constructive changes. When we engage our wildness in a conscious, contained way, we draw our sword; we use wrathful means to find our no. Anger is also our ally when expressing healthy outrage, for example, on behalf of the hurt inner child, where felt anger helps heal the consequences of an abusive childhood.

On the other hand, rage is anger gone rampant. Rage is expressed overtly or covertly, such as in emotionally abusive passive aggression, which is extremely destructive. Passive aggressive people may well deny their anger, or narcissistically 'believe' that everything is perfectly ok, and even that they are saints.

Addressing issues to do with the variables of how anger plays out in people's lives is almost always a relevant counseling and coaching theme in a reading. There are many pointers to the theme of anger in hands:

- Hard, inflexible hands - repressed emotions, potentially volatility
- Red, inflamed looking color of the skin - emotional strain
- White splotches in between redness - unexpressed anger
- Short fat water fingers with whorls - belligerence, bullying, control
- Thin, bent water fingers - mean streak
- White knuckles - can aspect suppressed rage
- Water lines spiky and messy - emotional and/or physical abuse, cruelty
- Venus mounts bulbous - temperamental, potentially volatile, demanding
- Bulbous Venus mounts on thin, hard hands - potential violence, cruelty
- Large Mars mounts - quick to anger
- Deep lines that ray from Mars mounts - easily inflamed

- Clenched fists - belligerence
- Courage loops - warrior-like reactions
- Large angles of dexterity - temper could suddenly flare
- Clubbed thumbs with simian lines - traditional sign of pent up, potentially murderous rage

Burnout

Clients who are suffering from burnout may not know that they have burnout. They share about constantly feeling physically and psychologically exhausted, depressed and pessimistic, of being void of any motivation, interest in or care about their work and of feeling totally uninspired by life. Increased alcohol or other drug intake is another symptom of burnout. If left unchecked, burnout has severe long-term physical, emotional, vocational and mental consequences.

Assist by learning about and explaining to clients what burnout syndrome is, and by unpacking and identifying the components of the internal and external stressors that have resulted in their burnout. Action steps to restore and replenish joie de vivre include meditation, breathwork, counseling, getting enough sleep, time management that allows for hobbies and fitness programs, conscious relaxation, unplugging from technology, setting better boundaries and prioritizing social and family time. Look for:

- Worry lines - chronic stress
- Soft thin hands - depletion, exhaustion
- Earth lines faint - struggles to cope, reduced stamina
- Many falling lines from earth lines - leaks of energy, disillusion
- Air lines overlap into two sections - a period of change
- Thin fine lines - inertia, low resources, run down
- Venus mount thin, flat - workaday existence, minimal life force
- Pale hands - lack of focus, depletion, tiredness
- Mars mounts flabby, diminished - defeat, listlessness

- Small thumbs - less focus on direction, fewer resources
- Bar lines on fingers - stress, depletion
- Dots on lines - inner stress, crisis

Courage

The theme of courage embraces physical and emotional courage, but also includes social courage, which is the courage we need to be our authentic selves. The topic of moral courage might also arise in readings; what is the right thing to do in a given situation. Themes related to the presence or lack of physical bravery, fortitude and strength, and the capacity for sustaining emotional, mental and spiritual courage in times of adversity emerge through:

- Courage loops - invite adventure, bravery, courage in adversity
- Double loops - upheavals, aspirations descend into disaster
- Mars mounts well-developed - faces up to challenges, attraction to risk
- Fire shaped hands - resilience, resourcefulness
- Firm hands - initiative
- Fire fingers long with spatulate tips – energy, adventure, takes risks
- Fire lines - resourcefulness, strength
- Soft thin hands - depletion, exhaustion
- Thin fine lines - inertia, low resources
- Pale hands - depletion, tiredness
- Mars mounts flabby, diminished - defeat, listlessness

Creativity

Since we are all creative in differing ways it's no surprise that our hands reveal not only different styles of creative expression, but also signal when our creativity is hampered. Creativity is significantly aspected in the hands of people with:

- Long fire fingers - extra energy, creativity, giving voice to the soul
- Whorls on fire fingers - classic sign of artist
- Peacock's eyes - artistic flair, design sense
- Tented arches - musicality
- Style loops - design sense, décor, attunement to colour
- Music loops – rhythm, loves music
- Upper minor water lines - appreciation of beauty, poetry, art
- Curves of creativity - creative concepts, inspiration, imagination
- Spatulate fingertips - creative, innovative, inventive, enthusiastic
- Air lines slope to Moon mounts - innovative ideas, creative perceptiveness
- Air lines wavy - imagination
- Minor air lines straight - spacial awareness, architecture, photography
- Vertical lines on Sun mounts - help flow of creative expression
- Pluto mounts dip into wrists - the dancer
- Angles of dexterity - good with hands and crafts
- Angles of time and harmony - music, dance
- Writer's forks - literary orientation, wordsmith
- Earth shaped hands - sculpting, pottery, gardens
- Sun mount triradius missing - blocks to creativity

Gambling

Gambling addiction and its widespread consequences is a theme that readers might regularly encounter. Sometimes one can intuitively pick up despair in a person who is in effect of a family member or partner's gambling addiction. In both the hands of the gambler and in those who are secondarily affected by the disease of gambling addiction, we look for:

- Whorls on long fire fingers - liking for high-risk activities
- Lower minor water lines, straight - craving for peak experience
- Earth shaped hands - laziness, wants the quick buck
- Fire shaped hands - attraction to risk and danger

Initiatives

An obvious component of all coaching practices is the supporting of clients to take action steps to manifest their goals. The topic of peoples' dreams, concepts, strategies and initiatives arises more often than not in readings. In this context I like to support by encouraging and hearing out their branding and marketing ideas, such as the relevance of symbolism in their logo, what name to brand under, website design suggestions, social media and any other ideas on how to out-reach their services.

Jealousy and Envy

Jealousy and envy are closely connected but differ slightly. Envy pertains to the desire for attributes, such as looks or status enjoyed by another. Jealousy often arises due to a relationship being threatened by a third person but can show up in many variables, such as in families where there is rivalry between siblings, or between parents and children. Examples include the mother who is jealous of her daughter, or a son who is jealous of his father. These emotions are deemed 'bad'; they are denied admission.

The tormenting emotion of the heart that is jealousy is part thought and part bodily sensation. Born of competition, the feelings intertwine with pain, resentment, bitterness, shame, despair, hopelessness, betrayal, anger at not matching up and fear of limited supply. For some people, jealousy paralyzes, it is too shameful to speak about and is suffered behind a mask, in a deeply private self-pitied and judgmental realm.

As a real emotion, when we retrieve the power of the emotional energy, we can transmute jealousy into a friend. Firstly, with honest admission. When we fully allow for our own longings and authentically feel into the sadness, grief and utter vulnerability of life's unfairness, space comes for blessing ourselves and the situation or person. Next is to stake claim to our capacity for appreciation and admiration, whether it be of beauty, money, or anything else. We change the lens; in viewing the situation through eyes of profound self-compassion and self-honoring, we feel more free.

Some signs in hands that might invoke themes of jealousy and envy are:

- Lower minor water line, straight - jealous, obsessive traits
- Stiff hands - controlling
- Fingers held tightly together - fear, insecurity
- Thumbs low set - domineering
- Thumbs straight - uncompromising, "sergeant major"
- Water fingers bent - emotional acquisitiveness, possessiveness
- Simian lines - control, intensity, obsession
- Attachment lines - dependency, neediness, insecurity

Joy

A poignant truth is that for many of us, it is as challenging to feel joyful as it is to be in emotional pain. Through commands in childhood such as "be quiet" and "behave" we have been educated out of spontaneity. Children wake exuberantly to the magic of existence, but being confronted with irritable or angry instructions from parents or teachers shuts down the very aliveness and joy that we are designed for. As sensitive children, the controlling and judgmental energies we encounter set in place a harsh inner critic. Unconsciously, happiness brings up feelings of fear on behalf of the terrified child that we once were, along with inner criticism. As adults, we feel joy, but we then instantly face another problem, the sense of being in trouble for being happy. This causes pain.

As counseling and coaching readers, we often encounter clients who simply cannot and don't want to be in their joy; for them joy is too scary. We cannot hold them in a happy place. They are unwilling and unable to allow themselves to fight for the gift of uncompromising happiness.

When the theme of how to be happy arises, consider sharing this quote from Elizabeth Gilbert:

"Happiness is the consequence of personal effort. You fight for it, strive for it, insist upon it, and sometimes even travel around the world looking for it. You have to participate relentlessly in the manifestations of your own blessings. And once you have achieved a state of happiness, you must never become lax about maintaining it. You must make a mighty effort to keep swimming upward into that happiness forever, to stay afloat on top of it."

Leadership

There are clear indicators in the hands of those for whom leading and motivating other people comes naturally. We quite easily see if they were placed in positions of authority from a young age, perhaps as head girl or boy or sport captain in school. The hands of people with personal magnetism, who have an air of command and who attract attention might have:

- Fire shape, firm - enterprising, energetic, enthusiastic, determined
- Jupiter mounts, large - ambition, aspiration
- Whorls on thumbs - the boss, efficacy, determination, authority
- Whorls on long fire fingers - expressive, showy
- Charisma loops - inspire loyalty, captains, prefects

- Serious intent loops - responsibility, accountability
- Water fingers long - leadership, others invest confidence
- Thumbs large - strength of character, resourcefulness
- Fingers held wide - openness, friendliness, charisma

Life Purpose

"The searching is the finding and the pursuit is the achievement."
Rabbi Dr. Abraham J. Twerski

Ikigai is a Japanese concept that means "a reason for being." Similar in meaning to the French phrase *"raison d'être"*, it describes a person's most important purpose or reason for living. In it are four components: that which you love, that which the world needs, that which you can earn from, and that which you're good at. Another metaphor for *ikigai* is "a sacred bundle" into which we gather our unique skill and message and from which we contribute to the world. It's in doing what we love that something in us rests in peace; we are in the 'zone', with a sense of having transcended time/space and a feeling of being 'on purpose'.

Finding meaning and purpose is a critical theme for many. When working to help a client to align with a vocational calling, helpful enquiry questions include 'What would you love?' "What activities do you get lost in?" and "When you were little, what did you dream of becoming when you grew up?" This is an effective way to listen for the voice of the soul, who in early childhood whispered the answer. Exploring this question helps younger clients to make study choices.

A favorite of many examples of how this enquiry question yields results was with a girl in her final school year who sought vocational guidance. In answer to this question, she shared that as a child, that she told her mother that she "wanted to be a hit woman for the Italian mafia." Our conversation led to her choosing university subjects of economics and business administration. Ten years later she'd become the first female futures trading broker in a big investment company. All the energy frequencies of danger, risk, skill, precision, confidentiality and exclusivity of the fantasy had manifested in her life path of financial management. Another example is the person who as a child wanted to be an actor and who goes on to become a trainer and facilitator; just as in the fantasy, they have their audience.

But this being said, for those who for whatever reason can't be 'bigger, better, faster', we reframe the meaning of the concept of life purpose. There is a bigger picture, an intrinsically interwoven backdrop that has to do with a wider and wiser understanding. The Shambhala Buddhism teacher Cynthia Kneen says: *"Purpose is the soulful confidence that what I am is worthwhile"* and *"true success is measured by the amount of authentic happiness we can feel in a day."* For people who have no apparent sacred bundle, the concept that 'purpose' is an in this moment state of inner being, that 'purpose' is a space of grace, acceptance and inner love, and in fact, is merely a sensation, is very comforting. What we are, who we are, with or without a calling, a passion, a mission or a vocation, still has meaning and purpose.

Sometimes what I offer by way of vocational guidance is dismissed by the seeker as not being a perfectly appealing enough. There are those who expect an orgasmic 'aha' bolt-of-lightning-style, perfect, blissfully loud-and-clear 'calling' to be evidenced in their hands. The limitations of perfectionism and idealism paralyze them; they are demoralized by the 49% or so of bread and butter grind that is part and parcel of nearly every job on the planet.

In another situation we might meet with a giant of academic or other know-how; the person has a string of degrees and is successful, but not satisfied. Material pursuits feel meaningless, they are miserable, unfulfilled and don't enjoy their work. Here the profound question: "What constitutes enoughness?" is key. We do need to work towards the 1% tipping point criteria, to choose and hear the inspired inner 'yes' that makes a vocational choice worthwhile, that keeps us breathing our yes into it.

A related topic that often arises in readings is that people present with a sense of shame that they are "a jack of all trades, but a master of none." This diminishing saying implies failure and not good enoughness and yet the person is genuinely more suited to a variety of skills than to being in the same job for 50 years. Not everyone is made for specialization. In exploring this theme, consider too that perhaps it doesn't matter if we don't finish what we start; what matters more is that we had enough curiosity to give it a try.

The binary analysis of element compatibility of hand shape and skin texture is a point of departure into establishing the type of vocational environment to which the person is best suited. Some hand features that relate to careers are:

- Earth shape - security industry, farming, nursing, catering, animals, civil service
- Water shape - fundraising, beauty, dance, public relations
- Fire shape - sport, film, wines, politics, acting, investments, army, mining
- Air shape - internet technology, media, academia, sales, engineering, homeopathy
- Earth skin - pottery, building, farming, landscaping, hospitality, nutrition
- Water skin - counseling, music, fine art, aromatherapy, sea
- Fire skin - surgery, mechanics, economics, armed forces
- Air skin - philosophy, research, medicine, writing, advertising
- Arches on many fingers - teaching, studying, academia, police
- Loops on all fingers - inspiration not aspiration, mediation, diplomacy
- Whorls - teaching, research, investigation, analysis, specialization
- Style loops - design, décor, fashion
- Humanitarian lines - activism, altruism, charity, ministry

- Upper minor water lines - special effects, gaming, beauty, poetry, art, devotion, ministry
- Straight minor earth straight, long - loyalty/devotion to one career
- Minor earth enters from Moon mount - social, service, people
- Air line long, straight - research, therapies, media, internet technology
- Water fingers long - leadership, authority
- Fire fingers long - creativity, sport, acting, movie directing
- Thumbs large - outdoors, manual
- Thumbs small - routine, repetitive
- Angle of dexterity - active profession, not desk bound

Personal Style

This is a theme that occasionally arises; topics of hair styles and colors, tattoos, the extent of their caring or not caring about their appearance are examples of what might be brought up. The client might share of poor confidence, or of being unhappy with their looks and ask for encouragement and opinion. As readers, we might motivate them to courageously express their unique personal style. Related palmar markings are:

- Style loops - admiration in the person of beauty elegance and of all things stylish
- Fire fingers long, with peacock's eyes - flair, own brand of

Post-traumatic (PTSD) and Complex Post-traumatic Stress Disorder (CPTSD)

PTSD is an anxiety disorder that develops after exposure to a terrifying ordeal in which physical harm to them or a loved one occurred or was threatened. Traumatic events such as violent personal assaults, natural or unnatural disasters, accidents, or military combat trigger PTSD. Symptoms include vivid flashbacks, as if the trauma is happening in current time, nightmares, sweating, nausea, shaking, disturbed sleep, hypervigilance, concentration issues, jumpiness and aggression. Trauma therapy is a specialized area; when a client presents with symptoms of trauma, we can help with listening and offering space for them to re-visit and tell us about what happened, and if need be, to refer them to a trauma counselor.

CPTSD differs from PTSD in that it accumulates over years as a result of prolonged interpersonal traumatization as children, as well as prolonged trauma as adults. CPTSD associates with narcissistic abuse, where emotional and/or physical pain or neglect was inflicted by attachment figures such as parents, older siblings or partners. The person is psychically, emotionally and mentally taken over, trauma-bonded, sucked empty and broken. CPTSD has lasting repercussions. Symptoms include difficulty with regulating emotions, melt-downs, anxiety and depression, shame, guilt, isolation and withdrawal, IBS, auto-immune and other illnesses, crippled self-esteem with acute self-criticism, severely lowered capacity to experience happiness and many others. CPTSD is extremely common and often undiagnosed. Clients who are or have been in narcissistically abusive relationships will feel greatly supported by readers who identify and unpack the component parts of this counseling and coaching theme.

- Pale hands - dismay, trauma
- Moist hands - rampant emotions
- Stars on water lines - shock

Self-sabotage

How regularly in our lives do we enact the opposite of creativity, self-sabotage? How does the masterminding of our own undoing play out in self-destructive thoughts, feelings, behaviors, obsessions and patterns? This enquiry regularly features in a chirology practice; many people struggle with subtle and devious and overtly damaging ways of hurting ourselves. This conversation interweaves with ways to up-level self-esteem and self-love.

Shock

Through careful examination of the hands and in dialogue we soon pick up on the situations in clients' lives that have caused shock. These might be in current time, or past. Sometimes a client doesn't realize they are in shock, but are suffering symptoms like exhaustion or brain fog. Help by reassuring that physical and emotional reactions are natural, normal, and to be expected. Look for:

- Star in water line - extreme emotional shock, trauma
- Falling lines from water lines - disappointment, dismay
- Trembling - distress
- Vitality
- The quality and quantity of people's joie de vivre, stamina and life energy is a big topic that very often arises in readings. We readily identify positive, life affirming traits in:
- Small firm hands - physically active, resilience
- Spatulate fingertips - enthusiasm, restless adventurousness
- Well-developed but firm Venus mounts - libido
- Firm, well-proportioned lower Mars mounts - energy, courage
- Fire lines - added energy
- Fire shaped hands, firm - restless, easily bored, live life to the max

More Fire Themes

Abuse
Ambition
Anger
Bites off more than can chew
Bullying
Burnout
Complex Post-Traumatic Stress Disorder (CPTSD)
Control
Courage
Creativity (ties to personal style) – is it hampered?

Cruelty
Envy
Exercise
Focus
Gambling
Hate crimes
High risk activity
Impatience
Impulsiveness
Initiatives
Intention
Jealousy
Joie de vivre
Joy
Leadership
Life Purpose
Military
Motivation
Optimal future
Overworked but underemployed or underproductive
Personal style - the courage to be me
Post-Traumatic Stress Disorder (PTSD)
Punishment
Rage
Recklessness
Revenge
Scorn
Self-importance
Self-sabotage
Sexual abuse
Sexuality
Shock
Skills
Sport
Staying power
Taking personal authority
Talents
Transformation

Trauma
Trauma bonds
Venom
Violence
Vitality
Will and willingness (to bring changes/adjustments)
Work – career - vocation
Workplace issues

Air Counseling and Coaching Themes

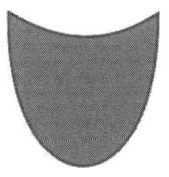

The Mental Realm

Intellect • Communication

Psychoanalysis

Education • Hobbies

In counseling and coaching with chirology, the realm of air encompasses these primary areas of human experience: communication (both expressed and subjective), the intellect, psychology, education, interests, hobbies, and the quality of our air governed emotions.

Anxiety

Air governs our nervous systems. From their hand prints we readily identify nervous system overdrive and the possibility of a client's suffering in a web of crippling anxiety. For many highly anxious people, depression interweaves. Susceptibility to, as well as full presence of anxiety, stress and worry is revealed by:

- Full hands with very many fine lines - Highly Sensitive People
- Shaky, tremoring hands - stress
- The gesture of wringing the hands - tension, worry
- Nails, bitten - anxiety, worry, insoluble dilemmas
- Moist skin, sometimes even just of the fingertips - chronic or acute stress situation
- Pale skin - fear
- Moon mounts, red - worry about family
- A cracked appearance of fingertip dermatoglyphics - longstanding stress
- Worry lines from Venus mounts ray across palms - worry

165

- Furriness in air lines; a section of the line has a cotton-wool appearance - sure sign of anxiety
- Excessive vertical or horizontal lines or ridges on nails - stress related biochemical imbalance
- Too many vertical (activation) and horizontal (bar) lines on fingers - hyperactivation of the nervous system

Communication

This is a very relevant air governed counseling and coaching theme; our clients' style of communication is intrinsic to every consultation. How do they articulate, are they talkative or reticent? How do they communicate subjectively, how in touch and honest, or repressed and in denial are they with themselves? We are alert to both outward and inward communication. When clients are evasive and avoid facing the truth, or don't want to speak, or speak over you, it is sometimes appropriate to directly address their communication styles in the conversation. Relevant hand features are:

- Fingers held wide - open communicator
- Fingers tightly held - reticence, shyness, mistrust, withhold
- Fire fingers long - strong persona, perhaps a façade
- Empty hands, few lines - thought and emotions kept private
- Air line curves upwards to Mercury - versatile, eloquent communicator
- Air lines clear - add eloquence
- Arches - reserve, caution, skepticism
- Humor loops - wry humor, sarcastic bent
- Air lines dip to Pluto mounts - curious, sleuth-like, investigative
- Narrowed quadrangles - secretiveness
- Minor earth lines doubled - hard to get to know, strong persona
- Air fingertips curve to fire - tactfulness, gentleness with spoken word, dislike being invaded

- Air fingers bend to fire - deceit, manipulation of communication, fondness for intrigue
- Air fingers long, held wide - tactlessness, enjoys exchange of ideas
- Fingers stiff - fixed in opinion
- Fingers closely held - reticence, guardedness, privacy
- Thumbs flexible, bendy - good mimic

Detachment

Detachment diminishes joy and inhibits intimacy and is linked to excess air in the psyche. Here we have two topic themes that often arise in readings; that of detachment in the client themselves, or the ramifications of detachment by the people in the client's life who disassociate.

Indications of this trait or situation show up in:

- Detachment lines, separated sections of air lines float on Uranus mounts - when immersed in an activity or train of thought, the person becomes very detached.
- Air shaped hands - preoccupation, disassociation from emotion
- Air fingers held wide - quick to feel restricted, needs space
- Phalanges, basal, narrowed - intellectualization, rationalization

Education

In the air realm, issues that have in the past or are in the present handicapping people's education often become a focus. The mental area of intellectual potential is an alive and challenging, even critical, realm in people who feel empty, despairing, unconfident and uncertain of how to further themselves. They are on the spectrum between being under or over-educated and suffering mental, emotional and financial consequences. Perhaps the work life of a client with a string of degrees is spiritless, or the opposite, the person feels inadequate; they are highly intelligent, but for a variety of possible reasons were formally uneducated. Damaging formative influences, such as teachers who humiliated or otherwise discouraged, or parents who couldn't afford to educate, are related topics. This conversation mostly opens through inquiry questions.

Guilt

"Guilt and shame are twisted sadness."
Lazaris

Guilt is a focus on behavior; something bad has been done and remorse results. Or, other's expectations haven't been lived up to, resulting in oppressive feelings of guilt. Either something is done that ought not to have been done, or something that we believe ought to have been done, has not been done. The feeling is driven by conscience and does not easily go away.

Air governed guilt has no substance, it is a self-punishing emotion that in essence is synthetic. Guilt keeps the past alive, it paralyses, numbs and disables functioning. As the 'junk food' of emotions, guilt might be hiding anger that we don't feel we have the right to have. Or, remorse becomes an expedient motivator; we act out of misplaced obligation. This then putrefies to resentment, and fosters self-pity.

Unpacking whether the person's remorse is authentic or justified is an area of enquiry that often arises in readings. Guilt can't be seen directly in the hands per se, but the theme emerges through dialogue.

Hobbies and Interests

This air governed realm of maintaining curiosity, of seeking furtherance and of the benefits of meditative immersion in hobbies often arises for people who have no interests whatsoever. They feel empty and have no enthusiasm. We enquire as to what it is that is handicapping them; do they doubt themselves, are they depressed, what is it that renders them incapable of looking at life through eyes of wonder? What set of circumstances might move them towards creative expression?

Others present with wanting to share about their skills and talents in the hobby realm, in which case the harmony of this realm is validated and affirmed. To open this conversation, look for:

- Air line dips to Moon mount - creative thinker
- Air line, straight - practical interests, research
- Air line, curves up - feel for financial markets
- Lines rising from air lines - many interests
- Tented arch dermatoglyphics – zest for interests, love of music
- Thumbs, angles of dexterity - craftsperson
- Deep straight minor air lines - spatial awareness, photography, architecture
- Style loops - design flair
- Peacock's eyes - art, creativity, imagination

Independence

The subject of self-reliance pops up in relation to various situations, such as with young home-leavers, in business and career situations and divorces. Look for signs of the call to independence in:

- Earth and air lines separate at their start - early self-reliance
- Fingers held wide - free-spiritedness
- Air fingers very wide spaced - extreme independence, separation

- Space between earth and fire fingers - inner security
- Earth fingers short - little regard for convention
- Whorls - original thinker, individualist
- Whorl on Moon mount - highlights emotional independence

Inner Critic (IC)

Our inner critic is an alive slavemaster whose voice is a thought that brings up feelings. IC attacks with unkind, even vicious inner dialogue. The IC's voice tells us to perform and achieve, or tells us "you'll never succeed anyway", which relieves us of trying. Its harsh style of motivation demands that we meet impossible standards and its function is to keep us 'safer' i.e. in the familiar repeated not good enough emotional state that we know and are (un)comfortable with. The majority of us struggle with the sense of our somehow never doing enough, so this theme arises more often than not.

Not to be underestimated, the inner critic is an old satanic force that appears to encourage unhappiness. This powerful entity that subtly possesses and runs many people's lives has a modus operandi that is full of contradictory rules about what is and isn't good enough.

A compassionate perspective to consider is that the inner critic is like an inner coach whose intentions are in fact benevolent; our inner critic wants us to do our best. Paradoxically, the inner critic wants to make us good enough to reach oneness with God, but wants nothing to do with the pain of emptiness. It wants to engage any strategy possible to avoid the hole inside (place of holiness) at all costs. Its job is to control painful feelings and to promote 'safe' but limiting behaviors. Nevertheless, there might be an underlying beautiful reason and positive intention for the message behind the inner critic's voice that expresses itself so inefficiently.

The IC resides permanently in our psyche. The longing of this sub-personality is for loving embrace and integration. Harnessing and managing the voice of the IC comes with understanding and

170

acknowledging the source of the voice. We assume dominion by consciously and intentionally choosing to meet our own standards.

Outward projected criticism is rooted in self-criticism; this is relevant both for those who present with feeling criticized by others and for those who experience themselves as being judgmental.

Criticism is appropriate and helpful when offered constructively, within context and with suggestions for confidence building and improvement, for example, when being evaluated in a work or sport environment. Relevant markings are:

- Earth fingers bend to fire - self-critical, pressurized by demands
- Knotty fingers - concern for detail and method, self criticism
- Fingers very thin - fussy, exacting, idealistic
- Earth fingers long - seriousness, studiousness, pessimism
- Upper minor water lines - own worst critic, exacting standards, idealism, nothing good enough, anxiety, conscience, discontent, despair, disappointment, only God will suffice
- Humor loops - jaded, cynical, bitter
- Whorls on air fingers - fixed opinions
- Radial loops on water fingers - exposure to criticism in childhood, sensitized to criticism, fears disapproval

Intellect

The intellect, along with its cousin intelligence, are themes which arise when we are endeavouring to optimally support clients' study and career choices. Through their hands, we see clues as to the person's style of thinking and types of thought process. Are they an intellectual and analytical type who resonates with raw, rational, factual and scientific logic, or does their thought process engage more emotional involvement, in the non-linear realms of intuitive

171

perception and inner knowing? To better understand their needs and preferences, look for:

- Air shaped hands - investigative, analytical, deliberating, psychological
- Air phalanges (fingertips) large - security in thinking, ideology, the search for impartial truth
- Whorls - analytical, seeker of explanations
- Whorls on air fingers - systematic organisation
- Fingers, knotty - philosophical, deliberates, examines, analyzes
- Air lines, long, straight - researcher, investigator
- Air lines, dip deep to Pluto - penetrative thinking, the investigative sleuth
- Air lines, doubled - thinks on two levels, mental dexterity
- Simian lines - potential ability to focus on research

Memory

The fear of loss of mental faculties is an extremely alive and troubling counseling and coaching theme for many. The topic of good long-term but weakening short-term memory often features in discussions of cognitive abilities. Examine:

- Air lines, end in islands - mental stress, forgetfulness
- Air lines, tassels, striations, frayed - memory loss, weakening cognition
- Memory loops - good long-term memory, perhaps poorer short-term memory

Mental Health

While mental health diagnosis is a vast arena that is beyond our scope of practice as readers, clients with mental health conditions do seek our services, so it is helpful to have at least a little insight into some of the maladaptive patterns of behavior and relating that affect people's lives.

Disorders commonly include but are not limited to: depressive, anxiety and panic disorders, trauma related stress disorders, obsessive-compulsive personality disorders (not the same as obsessive-compulsive disorder), addictive substance use and behavioral, such as food, gambling and sex related disorders, phobias, autism spectrum, attention-deficit/hyperactivity disorders, bipolar, narcissism, schizophrenia spectrum and psychotic disorders.

Clients who self-harm e.g. with cutting are exhibiting symptoms of borderline personality disorder (BPD, also known as emotional dysregulation disorder). Dangerously impulsive behavior is also characterized, as well as patterns of instability in interpersonal relationships, extremes of idealization and then devaluation of others, unstable moods and difficulty regulating strong emotional reactions. With consistent therapies, BPD is a treatable condition.

Occasionally a client might report of their challenges with a person close to them who is diagnosed with the serious and often untreatable antisocial personality disorder, where the person is exploitative, dangerous, disregards others, has no empathy or remorse, breaks moral and social codes, lies and gets onto the wrong side of the law.

Mental health disorders are clinically categorized into three groups; cluster A, B and C. Cluster A disorders are linked with social withdrawal, oddness, anxiety, paranoia, introspection, inhibition, feelings of inadequacy and difficulty forming relationships. Cluster B disorders are characterized by erratic, dramatic and unpredictable behaviours, impulsiveness, little regard for, or violation of, others' needs, lack of remorse, lack of impulse control and emotional regulation, self-harm, hysteria, need for attention, arrogance, empathy deficiency and sexual promiscuity. Cluster C categorizes disorders of dependency, perfectionism, fear, depression, avoidance, introversion, excessive fear of rejection and criticism, anxiety, pessimism, passivity and perfectionism. The diagnosis and symptoms of many of these conditions overlay and interweave with each other.

We do not attempt to diagnose mental health conditions but may be alerted by people's behavior, or they inform us of their diagnosis. Palmar features that relate to general mental health are:

- Air lines, broken - mental breakdown
- Air lines, doubled - mental dexterity, cranky, crazy, dualities
- Air lines, tasselled - weakening mental faculties
- Air lines, crossed by bars - mental crisis
- Air lines, drop steeply to Pluto mounts - fantasy world, agoraphobia, depression
- Air lines, furry - anxiety disorders
- Water lines broken - emotionally split off, emotions in compartments
- Water lines, triplicated - defence mechanisms
- Water lines with many falling lines - no boundaries, abuse
- Water lines, chained - instability, anxiety
- Whorls close to the tips of fingers - sense of isolation
- Thumbs - excessively large - brutality, anger
- Hard thin hands with puffy Venus mounts - cruelty

Obsessions and Compulsions

Obsessive-compulsive disorder (OCD) is defined as a mental illness that causes repeatedly recurring obsessive thoughts or sensations and the uncontrollable urge to do something repetitively, over and over again.

The lives of sufferers are infused with hours of exhausting thought and behavior, such as compulsive counting, washing, checking, picking at hair and skin, tidying, along with intense fear and worry.

We might on occasion meet with a sufferer of the full spectrum of both obsession and compulsion. This condition is managed rather than cured; we are best advised to refer to a cognitive behavioral therapist or psychiatrist who can assist with management strategies. OCD can't be diagnosed from hands, but we can see obsessive traits through:

- Lower minor water lines, straight - obsession, focus
- Knotty fingers - precision

Verbal Abuse

There are tell-tale signs in hands of people who have been exposed to and/or are particularly sensitive to verbal violence:
- A 'barbed wire' appearance to start of the earth and air lines - strife in childhood
- Slight inward curves of tips of air fingers - dismayed by ugliness of spoken word
- Joining lines between water and air lines - manners and protocol high in value system
- Humor loops - sarcasm

Writing and Literary Talent

How to identify literary talent, the wordsmith or bookworm who does or will benefit immensely from journaling and writing? These are potential accurate indicators:
- Air lines, diverging forks at ends - 'writer's forks', seeing from different perspectives
- Earth fingertips bend to fire - the scribe
- Air skin texture - curiosity, love of reading
- Whorls - thinkers, researchers

More Air Themes

ADD
ADHD
Alzheimer's
Anxiety
Bitterness
Communication
Compulsions
Constantly shifting objectives
Criticism
Cynicism
Detachment
Education
Guilt
Hobbies
Human Rights
Independence
Inner critic
Intellect
Intelligence
Law
Learning
Media (and kid's exposure)
Memory
Mental Health
Obsessions
Post-traumatic Stress
Disorder
Psychology
Racism, bias, discrimination
Rebelliousness
Sarcasm
Self-Criticism
Sleep
Spatial Awareness
Stress

Unconventionality
Verbal Abuse
Worry
Writing and literary talent

Aether Counseling and Coaching Themes

The Spiritual Realm
Religion • Spirituality
The Non-Material Domain

The areas of human experience which are encompassed in the realm of aether are specific to the non-material; here we are tapping into matters to do with consciousness, spiritual perspectives, divinity, religious background, current beliefs, intuitive abilities, prayer and meditation, dreams, higher selves, channeled messages from beyond the veil, ritual, other lifetimes, angels and spirit guides.

Addiction

Attempts to self-regulate with substances and behavior patterns and with actions that come before other relationships commonly present as a critical theme in people's lives. Through the lens of the realm of aether, all addiction is sourced in "divine discontent", in the acutely empty hole in the soul that so longs for oneness with God.

In active addiction, our hungry ghosts clamor furiously for more, more, more, but as the 12 Step Program teaches, when attempting to self-soothe loneliness, anxiety, despair and other painful feelings with actions and substances, one will always be too many, and a thousand never enough.

The concept of hungry ghosts stems from several eastern traditions that refer to consequences of actions and to levels of suffering after death. Today the term is used to describe the hell-like realm of living with the insatiability of addiction. Nothing outside of us can fill the aching hole of our existential longing.

Compassionate identification of and enquiry into intergenerational and childhood sources of addictive patterns and their consequences, both in the life of the client, as well as for those in effect of addicts in their family constellation, might begin with the energies which exude from:

- Lower minor water lines, straight - craving for peak experience, addiction in lineage
- Lower minor water lines, curved - allergic responses to what the body craves
- Air lines very faint – unsteady mind
- Full, plump water phalanges - comfort sought from external material sources
- Pads of fat on backs of phalanges – indulgence
- Fingers thick - greed
- Long fire fingers with whorls - attraction to risk, perhaps gambling
- Clammy hands - alcohol excess
- Bluish nails – smoking
- Tremors

Aging

Clients who have entered their eldering years often present with questioning how they might come to terms with the ramifications of aging. On the aether level of this large and diverse counseling and coaching theme, we could discuss how to embrace the natural order of seasons, how to compassionately honor the winter of our life, and how to receive growing old as both a gift and a responsibility.

Considering conscious aging in the air level might mean articulating a philosophy for how to live our late chapter, how to meet the inevitable with acceptance, curiosity and trust, and what our legacy might be. Pertinent to the fire level is how to disengage from doing and the often very challenging issue for many; the question of how to sustain a sense of purpose and meaning after retirement. Involvement in service to others and social participation is a water level function of graceful eldering. On the earth level, we discuss family, how to slow physical decline, how to manage bodily discomforts, and how to maximize pleasure and financial security.

Crisis

Life crises can occur within any of the 5 Realms. Types of crisis include survival crisis (earth), health crisis (earth), self-pity/negative ego crisis of "I'm a failure, I'm not good enough" (water), manipulative crisis, as in fury at not getting your way (water), grief of loss (water), the often extremely terrifying success crisis (fire) and the dark night of the soul of a spiritual (emergency) crisis.

Crisis brews invisibly, then breaks and spills into reality; the consequences spread and cause damage. When in crisis, things are happening too fast, it is impossible to process or assimilate the demands of the situation, which feel too big. There is paralysis, inability to respond, integrate or cope, daily routine is disrupted, we feel mentally and emotionally broken.

Eventually, what felt critical retreats, and finally ends in a natural conclusion, but amidst the phases of crisis is a sense of there being a vacuous space; that the crisis will last forever.

Once these criteria are defined, we can guide the client into strategic steps towards strengthening and healing. We can assist by encouraging them to use their crisis to jump start and catapult themselves forward. As painful as crisis is, within the changes lies innate opportunity, meaning, significance and value. Crisis in people's lives might be suggested by:

- Stars on water lines - shock, emotional pain
- Breaks in any main line - critical significance pertaining to the meaning of the line
- Perspiring fingertips - current time crisis
- Tremoring hands - stress

Death

Clients who present with terminal illness each face their own unique set of complex emotions and circumstances. The consequences of their situation is far-reaching and, for most people, terribly difficult to come to terms with. Therapy with a dying person must be focused on helping them to communicate their needs and to support them with what is often a vast range of emotional and practical challenges, including preparing for pain. This is a specialized field; therapists are encouraged to personally confront their feelings around death before engaging with a dying client.

Depending on where they are on the spectrum of functioning, acceptance and readiness to meet their death, the client might find much comfort in your coaching them with formulating a legacy letter. Another name for a legacy letter is an ethical will; it is a spiritual document that is unrelated to material wealth distribution. As a non-legal document, legacy letters are written to share values, life lessons, hopes, dreams, love, forgiveness, blessings and anything else. Legacy letters may be short or long. The format is simple; context, story, lessons learned and blessings. We begin with the context of where we are at currently. Next is the story of what is relevant to our life that we'd like others to know about; this includes practical issues and any requests we might have, and continues with any words of wisdom and guidance that we'd like to impart. Legacy letters end with our blessings of love.

There are no specific chirological indicators of death in hands. The old superstition of a short life line evidencing early death is a myth;

short life lines relate more to how we interface with life rather than to any chronological event.

Themes of religion and spirituality, health and the stages of grief intermingle with death and dying.

Dreams

We dream in different ways, such as day dreaming and fantasy, but it's our clients' deep state dreams, another aether governed topic, that readers are often asked about. We might try to unravel and deepen into meanings for the symbolism in remembered dreams with clients. Look for:

- Memory loops - vividly symbolic dreams, clear recall, intuitive gift for dream interpretation
- Double loops - strengthen intuitive faculties
- Upper minor water lines - vivid fantasy

Intuition and Psychic Ability

This is a theme that arises more commonly than not; most people are curious about extra-sensory perceptions. Everyone is intuitive, but we might enter this theme via:

- Water shaped hands - receptive, intuitive
- Fingers taper to relative pointiness at their tips - antennae, feelers that pick up vibrational frequencies, vision, inspiration
- Bows of Intuition - psychic and mediumistic ability
- Memory loops - active intuitive perceptions
- Rings of Solomon - spiritual attunement, wisdom
- Double loops - increase psychic sensitivity
- Neptune mounts, raised - attunement to non-material realms

Meditation

As with prayer, many clients speak about the role of meditation in their lives. Meditation is receiving; sitting or lying down in a pocket of stillness, aligning, plugging into and logging on to the infinite, we listen and respond to our inner voice of discovering, hearing or knowing. As a God-given resource, meditation brings peace; everyone should meditate. In meditation, we access and connect with the eternal, the vast and allowing spaciousness that embraces all that is.

Past, Parallel and Future Lives

Some clients are significantly drawn to exploring possibilities within this theme; for them other lifetimes feel very real. They have awareness of, or look to consider that past, parallel or future life experiences might be bleeding through the dimensions and influencing this lifetime.

Quantum science teaches that all existence is holographic. What we experience as our present time reality is happening simultaneously in different dimensional frequencies. Time does not exist; it is a unit of geological chronology defined and named "time" by man. This system of measurement has been superimposed upon eternal, timeless presence. Our thoughts function independently of or beyond space/time, therefore all experience, (i.e. our birth and death, past, parallel and future lives) exist concurrently in past, present and future simultaneously in universal oneness. Features in hands that might draw us into discussion about other lifetimes are:

- Upper minor water lines - often seen on monks and nuns, lifetimes questing for the exalted, only God will suffice
- Angel protection (sister/support) lines on the insides of earth lines - awareness of spiritual realms
- Memory loops - memories, dreams, non-material awareness

Prayer

Many clients seek to share about the role of prayer in their lives. Prayer is asking. As we pray, we connect to and work with divinity. Our attention shifts from what divides us to what unites us; active prayerfulness is a means by which to assist personal and global transformation. Consider how saying grace at mealtimes and praying together in meetings strengthens bonds. Through the lens of aether consciousness, when we meet our Creator with our broken hearts and ask for help we will be guided, protected and directed.

Protection

Feeling the need for psychic protection is a theme that regularly arises especially for people from several cultures who have strongly intractable beliefs in cast spells, black magic and demonic spirit possession. How to assist clients who believe they are being psychically invaded by entities and who need support for their fears?

From an ethical perspective, this counselling and coaching theme ought be handled carefully and with discretion, but it remains vital that we meet our clients where they are. If someone says they believe their mother-in-law has cast a spell upon them, we honour them by holding presence, listening, not judging or offering viewpoints that contradict or in any way marginalize or minimise the intensity of their subjective experience. Based upon personal beliefs and preferences, readers are at liberty to suggest prayer, banishing or other rituals, ceremony or magic spells.

Protection from threat of violence might require encouraging clients to get help from friends and authorities, to get a restraining order, to go 'no contact,' or to move away. Lines in hands that relate to themes of protection and spiritual support are:

- Fire lines on inside of earth lines - unseen friends, angelic protection, spiritual guides

Psychic Contracts and Leaks

For many, the sense of being psychically bound by cords or even chains, of being uncomfortably tied to, attached and contracted in with people to whom we leak energy is very real. This is a big topic that interweaves with addiction, sexual and other forms of abuse, co-dependency, abandonment, illness, shame, victimhood, resentments and with personal philosophies, but for those who present with this awareness, the feeling is debilitating in intensity. There might be a constant sense of being tired and drained, as if energy is leaking away. Boundaries are unclear; where do I end and others begin?

The phenomenon occurs in non-structured realms and includes the possibility of past-life bleed throughs, where experiences of other lives enter through permeable auric fields and influence current-time reality. While some cords can be positive, those who feel they are leaking energy will find suggestions of how to cut cords and of how to use other banishing rituals helpful.

Religion and Spirituality

In the context of the 5 Realm model, at least some mention with every client about their formative and current religious and spiritual situations, beliefs and preferences is a non-negotiable component; without conversing about the quality of their religious and spiritual life a chirology reading is incomplete.

From a spiritual crisis of feeling abandoned by God to deep connection with the higher power of their understanding, where are they on the spectrum of possibilities? Many people have deep faith and live according to higher beliefs, but it's astounding how many others are wounded in this realm.

Due to childhood double standards, punitively enforced religion, dismaying experiences with priests, rabbis, gurus and imams, or for any other reason, people are disillusioned and spiritually adrift. Many a time, people are cynical, angry and resentful towards God;

they feel cheated, wronged, hurt, abandoned and alone. They have no sense of a higher power; this can be a lonely path.

Signs in hands that directly relate to religious and spiritual matters include:

- Rings of Solomon - capacity of innate wisdom, insight, intuition
- Mystic cross - "old soul", wisdom seeker, advanced psychic
- Translucent skin - spiritual person
- Fire (influence) lines on insides of earth lines - spiritual support

Ritual

"Ritual is the formula through which harmony is restored."
Thomas Moore.

Clients present with an array of situations where they engage in, or might be well-advised to practice some form of ritual or ceremony. On the broad spectrum of possibilities is something as simple as how a candlelit bath in scented water soothes. For some clients, a daily devotional practice is relevant. Weddings, funerals, types of baptisms and initiations are daily life rituals. In the metaphysical realm, we might for instance ritual for protection, peace and healing, for gratitude or creativity, for manifesting money or a beloved, for the solstice, or anything else.

In South Africa, people, especially those from cultures where spells and magic are customary, regularly ask questions about how to protect themselves. In these readings, I include teaching clients what I have learned of how to perform protection and banishing rituals.

185

Spiritual Guides

The presence of spirit guides is another topic that regularly arises in readings. Our conversation might lead to speaking of clients' feeling the presence of angels, ancestors, grandparents, parents, children, animals and other unseen friends who have passed, or of totem animal guides, Higher Selves and other high level spirit guides with whom they communicate.

Many clients want to convene with guides but don't know how; they are interested in the spirit world and ask about methods for contacting and communing with a guide. They have a strong sense of the life in unseen realms, are open to visualization and to cultivating their awareness. Some spiritual readers practice assigning guides; they draw or describe and name the guide's identity. Chirology readers might consider facilitating or recommending a meditative guided visualization to invoke and acknowledge the presence of unseen friends; these may appear as human or animal and with surprising clarity about their gender, name and attire. Reading, understanding and respecting the images, metaphors, smells and other senses that one or many guides impart to us takes practice; in time, communing with them can be experienced in vivid detail.

In my practice, I've also met clients with schizoaffective disorder, a mental health condition that is a study in itself, but in this context, symptoms can include both delusion and mania. These clients have shared of terrifyingly extreme and harmful encounters with fallen angels and other demonic entities who have "guided" them towards their near demise.

- Fine lines parallel to earth lines on Venus mounts – angelic protection, spirit guides

Suicide

In a busy practice, this theme that so requires delicate navigation might arise more often than one might expect; many are in spiritual crisis and longing for deep acceptance, for rest, and for home.

We support this person by validating the place where they are right now, by being present to their crisis, their nightmare and to their cry for love. Their ancient pain is as old as humanity. They long for intimate connection but can't find it in this life. They long to live but don't know how.

Lending full presence says more than words ever could; not as therapists or specialists, but as friend to friend. We hold their hands, show them they are not alone. Whether they will live or die, we meet them now, in that strange place of not knowing. Even though right now they feel like leaving, touch them with life. Remind them that deep human connection is possible, here, in this life, in this moment. Offer your deep listening and simple reflection.

Whether they stay or go, they are healing in the only way they know how. We do not try to stop them feeling what they are feeling, cheer them up or tell them that everything is really okay. We meet them in their aloneness without trying to fix them, and without trying to convince them that their desire to die is wrong, sick or invalid.

Use gentle clarification questions; What brings you to me, were you referred? Who else are you speaking to? What other support do you have? Does the person who is supporting you know you are here with me? What are you looking for by coming to me? How serious is this? Have you tried suicide before, bought a gun, shored up tablets? Listen for, and reflect back any useful information.

Very importantly when sitting with a suicidal client is to check inside, what is happening with me? You are going where perhaps nobody else has dared to go, and in so doing, you meet yourself. Am I supposed to do this or not? Can I go to the depths with them? Can I meet my fears? If I as therapist am contracted and scared, I am the wrong person for them. Tell them this. Be authentic. You don't have to know how to fix or save them.

- Air lines that curve steeply downwards - traditional sign of suicidal thought
- Bent earth fingers - depressive traits
- Upper minor water lines - impossible standards, wants a perfect world

More Aether Themes

Addiction, also to sadness, anger, shame and pain
Aligning, listening and responding to your inner voice of knowing
Angels
Banishing
Calibrating
Ceremony
Chakras
Channelling, verbal and energetic
Clairaudience
Claircognizance
Clairsentience
Clairvoyance
Consciousness
Cord cutting
Death
Detached compassion
Dominion
Dream - recall and interpretation
Dying
Enoughness
Every act of a lower nature is a cry for love
Extra-sensory perceptions
Higher Self
Hungry ghosts

Intuition

Joyful-sorrow

Magic

Manifestation

Meditation

Openness to guidance from non-material realms

Other life bleed-throughs

Past/parallel/future lives

Personal mastery

Prayer - work with your divinity. Ask! and it will happen

Precognition

Premonition

Protection techniques

Psychic ability

Psychic leaks

Psychometrics

Radionics

Religion

Remote viewing

Retrocognition

Ritual

Scanning

Soul fragmentation and retrieval

Spells

Spirituality

Split-offs

Success – fear of

Suicide

Telekinesis

Telepathy

The occult

The subconscious

The unconscious

Time

Vulnerability is strength

Wisdom

Air

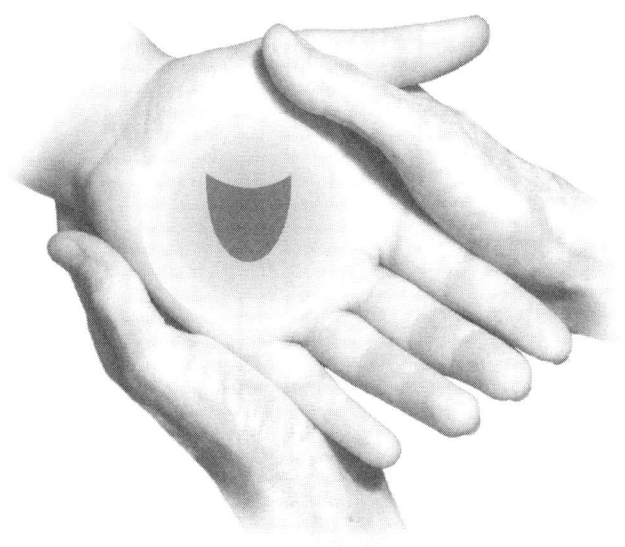

Design ~ Communication

AIR ~ DESIGN ~ COMMUNICATION

Observation

Online scheduled appointments don't provide any auditory information, but when clients call to schedule a reading, we might in their voice notice nuances of skepticism, or depression, or mention of their work or family; in a sense, this is where a reading begins.

For online readings, we rely a great deal more on intuition, while during in-person meetings we have more visual windows of perception. Every nuance of general posture and hand gesture informs.

From the get-go, take notice of how the client presents physically. When they arrive, notice their posture and manner of walking. What does their body language reveal? How do they carry their hands? Take note of the size of their hands in relation to their height. Are they wearing rings and if so, on which digits?

Look into their eyes, are they in physical and/or emotional pain? Are their eyes dull or bright, happy or worried, what energy radiates from their eyes? What is the general facial expression? Are they uncomfortable with eye contact, reserved, or looking everywhere except into your eyes?

What does their hand shake tell you? How do they respond to your outreached hand? Are they shy, or assertive? How does their handshake feel and what energy exudes to you? What does the consistency feel like, are the hands hard, or mushy? In this initial physical contact of their handshake style, much is revealed.

When seated, what does their body language reveal, do they lean back and slouch in the chair, or even turn their body away? What might this suggest? Do they sit stiffly upright on the edge of the chair, or even lean noticeably far forward towards you? Are they tense or relaxed?

Do they keep their hands hidden in their pockets, or folded together in their laps, or do they offer them splayed openly and generously? Do you notice any nervous movements like wringing or tremors?

Do they read the indemnity form carefully, perhaps ask for further explanation, or do they sign without reading? What is the person observing, what is their reaction to you and your environment, are they interested, do they look around, do they comment?

When printing the hands, be alert to the first feature that you detect. When you take their hands, look at them and stroke them, what jumps out? What is their skin texture, color and temperature? Do they have warts, moles, scars or calluses? What is their predominant hand shape? Here we do an initial observation of outline angles and curves of the hands, the size and flexibility of the thumbs, the nails, fingertip shapes, any fingers that are noticeably bent, thick or thin, the hollows and the mounts, and the depths of lines.

Listening

"When a person realizes he has been deeply heard, his eyes moisten. I think in some real sense he is weeping for joy. It is as though he were saying, "Thank God, somebody heard me. Someone knows what it's like to be me."
Carl Rogers

During chirology consultations, the reader, especially in the early minutes of the reading, assumes the more verbally active role. Our words comfort, evoke and invite, but readers who for the entire session assault clients with a monologue, who don't stop talking long enough to listen, will leave their clients feeling disappointed; they have not been heard. It is essential to balance the channeling of our spoken words with pausing. Allow space for what is most important for the person to be shared.

When to speak and when to listen is a delicate navigation that is key to providing an optimal experience for our clients. The quality of our listening influences the depth of our rapport. When sitting with a client, sensing (listening) with intuition yields source information more effectively than does cerebral analysis. By coming into the moment mindfully, with calm and patient relaxation into the heart of the other, good listeners hold a balance of conscious internal stillness with external engaged presence, which encourages opening.

The act of listening is multidimensional; we listen audibly, while also listening intuitively with spacious and loving hearts and all our senses. We maintain eye contact, listen attentively to gesture and body language for non-verbal communication and for the unsaid emotions and thoughts that live inside and in between words.

Truly skilled listening is an action of generosity, it is an alchemical activity of lending focused Presence, and in so doing, communicating empathy. It is the receiving of the person completely that enables them to receive themselves completely.

- At what level and with which type of awareness do we listen; are we really listening at all? How much of our listening is filtered through our autobiographical past experiences, viewpoints, prejudices, attitudes and beliefs? Do we have the intention to really understand, or are we concerned with what we want to say next?

- When clients interject while we as the reader are speaking, we make way for them to speak; we put our flow of thoughts and words on hold.

- Mostly, when clients are speaking, we give them time and do not interrupt them. But when they veer off course into laborious details of their storyline, interruption with a clarifying question or other technique is required.

Filtered Hearing

Clients sometimes hear what they want to hear. For example, I asked a client a very generalized question, "what happened with your father?" The person responded as if I had been extremely accurate; he thought I'd picked up his father's retrenchment and subsequent depression and replied, with much emotion, with the story of what had transpired with his Dad.

But that wasn't what I'd meant. In fact, my intuitive sense, which I wasn't sure was accurate, was that the father had died, which is why I couched the question so generally. He unconsciously interpreted what was actually said as a means of subjectively validating for himself that I as reader accurately 'saw' the situation.

This common psychological phenomenon of filtered hearing was verified in a research experiment. An American psychologist named Bertram Forer did a personality test for 39 students, afterwards giving them each an identical analysis report; almost all found their reading to be accurate. Filtered hearing is also called the 'Barnum effect', named after an American entertainer who observed how people gave high accuracy ratings to his descriptions of their personality and lives, when in fact the words he used were non-specific to them and general enough to apply to a wide range of people.

While sceptics perceive hand readers as being hucksters who con people with the gift of the gab, in my understanding filtered hearing is innocently sourced in deep vulnerability and in the need to feel understood. Providing the reader isn't out to exploit the person and is coming from a place of compassion and kindness, there is no inherent wrong-doing on the part of the reader who blends generalized terminology into their style of reading. Clients, especially those who are themselves empathic, tend to subjectively validate our accuracy through filtered hearing; this response is an intrinsic component of the hand reading craft.

Clients Who Insist on Staying in Their Story

Some clients are so set on narrating their story that they speak almost non-stop through the consultation. Insistently fixed on telling many details, they refuse to budge from deconstructing the who, when, why and what of the situation in every detail. They are controlling, and become resistant and even resentful or hostile when you interject with counseling guidance, observations, a different perspective or a suggestion. Any enquiry question that might help them to disidentify from their problem focused storyline falls on deaf ears.

Your invitation to them to participate in any somatic process that will help them to drop into their body and to feel into the underlying emotions of what is really going on at the heart of the matter is met with refusal. They are in their heads, and strongly identified with the drama of the situation.

How do we readers navigate this, how do we both meet them as they are, and at the same time do our work as a reader? The art of skilful interruption is a delicate matter. Some suggestions are:

- Interject with the hard truth. Articulate the observation that while you understand the importance of their sharing their story, that when they re-listen to the recording they might feel dissatisfied with the reading, or critical of themselves for having talked so much and that no space was left for receiving the potentially interesting and supportive chirological reading that they came for.

- Intrude with a strong request for clarification, such as "Help me to understand what is important here, what specifically is at the core of this challenge you have?"

197

- Reflect with empathy. Share with them that while you understand that the situation cuts deep, is painful, difficult, traumatic, frightening for them, you can't help change it, but that if they participate, that perhaps, if they are open to the possibility, you can offer a fresh perspective.

- Go to the body. Ask:" If you were me and I were you, in your body, what would I be feeling, and where am I feeling it?"

- Redirect them by persistently asking:" How was that for you?" "How did you feel when that happened?"

Unfortunately, some clients are incapable of changing their mind-sets and behavioral patterns; they spend years or a lifetime analyzing their situations every which way, obsessed with the analysis, with seeking sympathy and with an entrenched neediness that the when, what and who of their story will somehow eventually be perfectly understood. Sadly, they go from one therapist, doctor, reader or psychic to another, but their fixed identification with their storyline overrules any willingness to change.

Do I Speak about Myself?

Self-disclosure, where the counselling and coaching chirologist shares their personal experience and feelings, is often sourced in genuine empathy. The reader's sentiments are well-intended, but for the most part, clients don't feel supported by their reader speaking about themselves. While very occasionally it's appropriate to empathize with "I understand what you mean because I've been there" type feedback, most clients don't need or want to know that you as their reader can relate to their situation. Good listening does not mean saying to the person "I can relate", in fact it is very abandoning and annoying for the client when a reader keeps referring back to him/herself, or their experiences with other clients or life situations. The reader's need to share tends to make it about them.

As a general rule, it is better to not self-disclose, unless there is a pressing need that cannot be met in any other way, for example, referencing your personal life experience can be cognitively used as a technique to bring the client back from extreme self-absorption.

Minimize self-disclosure and be highly discerning about talking about yourself. It's far more supportive to directly summarize, clarify and feed back what they actually said. Keep communications specifically focused on their story; if you as a reader do choose to speak about your own experience, or to draw a parallel by relating the experience of another person you know, be sure that the content is relevant and helpful.

Repertoire

Each individual practitioner's style of delivery is molded from respective areas of their education, research, life story, culture, beliefs, interests and orientations. As professionals, we aspire to avoid stagnation through learning ways to up-level our intuitive, listening, observation, counselling, coaching and other skills.

With practice, experience and time, our techniques organically shape-shift, but at the same time, especially over many years of sustaining a professional practice, we find that elements of deliberately structured, methodical and repetitive repertoires are unavoidable.

We know what works. In my practice, as the counselling or coaching themes arise, I often find myself saying the same words, explaining the same concepts, and using the same repertoire of techniques, over and over again. When offering many readings, the use of my repetitive repertoire can sound stagnant, boring and worrisome to me, but the words, concepts and techniques that I offer are fresh for the client.

Terminology

Professional readers are well-advised to be careful with using diagnostic labels like psychotic, psychopathic, sociopathic, schizophrenic, manic depressive, bi-polar, narcissistic, narcopathic etc. unless they have an at least reasonably educated understanding of these disorders.

We also avoid prefacing sentences with "But" and for the most part, avoid asking the 'closed' question "Why?"

Counseling and Coaching Techniques

Asking

It's ok to ask questions to clarify our understanding of what the client is experiencing. While occasionally we meet with a client who expects us to be an all-knowing oracle and replies to a question with "you tell me", asking mostly helps people to deepen into feelings around the situation. We don't interrogate with too many questions, but in gently asking permission to better understand, we empower clients with space to direct the conversation. Inquiry questions are prefaced with what, how, how come; these are open questions which facilitate a free and open spaciousness for response.

Examples of open questions are: "What is most important for you in your life?" "What is the situation?" "How does it feel in your body? Can you allow?" "What do you perceive as being possible?" "What changes would you like to make, what action steps?" "How might you support yourself?" "What's the worst that can happen?" "What is possible, probable, inevitable?"

Avoid asking "why" questions. Why questions feed the analytical mind and pull people out of what they are feeling and into their thinking. While "why" can be useful, it is also deadly in that it triggers association with childhood "Why did you do that!" type parental disapproval. Why questions contain a connotation of criticism or judgment, cause contraction and evoke guilt, defensiveness and a sense of having to justify.

Being Trauma-Informed

Trauma-Informed Care (TIC) is an approach in the human service field that recognizes and acknowledges that people are more likely than not to have a history of trauma, the effects of which underpin their behavioral health problems. This awareness facilitates the shift in perspective from "What is wrong with this person?" to "What has happened to this person?" Without using a trauma-informed approach, the possibility of triggering or exacerbating trauma symptoms and re-traumatizing the client increases.

For readers, the guiding principles of Trauma-Informed Care, which include safety, trust and transparency, are helpful and relevant.

Bottom Lining

Often a burning issue arises at the beginning of the consultation. To stay present with the client and grounded in their situation, reflect the main theme back to them periodically throughout the reading. Notice it, condense and crystalize it by naming it out loud. Reconnect them by staying with the heart of the matter. What is their primary concern, what is most important for them? Bottom lining is about helping the person to get to the point, to the core of the burning issue.

Challenging

Any self-imposed limits that clients appear to have set for themselves might be challenged by an astute counseling and coaching chirologist; perhaps the person can deal with more than they think they can.

Championing

This is a wonderful technique that is especially important for those who have had a deficit of acknowledgement, approval and love, or who lack feedback. Championing is affirming the person's positive attributes, skills and talents. By letting them know that we see them in a positive light, we help them to feel more confident and to progress; we champion their resourcefulness, creativity, strengths and assets.

Clarifying

Repeatedly paraphrasing and clarifying the theme of the conversation and the situation, along with asking if we have properly understood feels affirming for clients and adds to their sense of being fully heard.

Goal Setting

Goal setting in traditional coaching is a creatively pro-active collaboration that is goal-focused on possibilities, on clearly identifying and outlining the person's intentions and then working out behavioral strategies and schedules. Coaches hold their clients accountable; the commitment to prioritize day-to-day recovery-related action steps is established. Creative goal setting is a more imaginative and artistic approach which invites in, and co-creates with, the raw materials of desire, imagination and expectancy. By consciously energizing our desires with these three alchemical ingredients, our goals have nowhere to go but into manifestation.

Immediacy

Keeping communications specific and focused on facts and feelings of relevant concerns, while avoiding tangents, generalizations, abstract discussions, or talking about others rather than the client.

Making Distinctions

When clients present with entangled situations which for them feel like facts, we assist by separating the component parts of what they perceive to be one, often limiting and disempowering fact or belief.

Mindfulness

Mindfulness based counseling is the conscious, non-judgmental and curious awareness and observation of present moment experience. The practice is relaxing in that it helps clients to drop inwards and engage with their thoughts, emotions and physical state from the perspective of a reflective observer.

Nonviolent Communication (NVC)

This inspiring teaching is structured around authentic communication, receptive, empathic listening and self-compassion. NVC outlines a four-part sentence-structured communication model.

- Observation: Make a non-evaluative statement that states only the accurate facts of the situation. "I've noticed that you haven't called for a while."
- Feeling: Authentically express feelings. Separate them from thoughts and evaluations. "I'm feeling anxious and vulnerable about our relationship."
- Need: Expressing a need is a tool to introduce honesty. "You are important to me and I need to feel close again."
- Request: Make a clearly worded request without expectations; the person may not be willing to comply. "Please can we meet up to talk?"

This highly recommended study is an invaluable aid for helping both clients and readers to communicate genuinely, honestly and respectfully in all areas of their lives.

Pausing

There is mediocrity in readings where the reader speaks non-stop, where they assail their clients with a barrage of wordy information without offering space for their client to share. As readers, we are well-advised to become comfortable and strong in holding useful silence. In holding an empty space and allowing time for what is most alive in the client to emerge, we give them time to assimilate and to speak. Quietness hastens positive outcome. Listen to silence as well as to words; silence gives the client control and space to take the helm and to guide the content and pace of their chirology experience. Silence is often the client's golden opportunity for authentic sharing.

Recovering

Is noticing and pointing out; we voice out loud any of the client's disconnected thoughts and dialogue that veers off point and then reconnecting the threads to bring the conversation back into alignment with the essence of the issue at hand.

Reframing

Reframing is a strategy used in therapy to help create a shift in perspective. Thoughts and ways of looking at a situation, person, or relationship that are based on emotion-driven reaction and which are rooted in old patterns that no longer serve might be seen through a different lens, recast and infused with renewed possibilities.

Summarizing

Summarizing is a way of paraphrasing, of summing up the essence of what is most alive for the person. Through artfully listening and then mirroring back, rapport deepens. Summarize with the energy, tone, speed and gestures of the person; this way they will feel you are fully present with them. Give feedback – "What I heard you say is....."

Transference ~ Countertransference ~ Projection

Transference describes how people unconsciously redirect their feelings, expectations or desires and apply the characteristics to someone else. For example, we easily perceive fatherly or motherly qualities in a new boss or partner and we transfer unrealistic expectations of protection and nurturing onto them. Transference is very common in all human interactions.

As readers, we encounter many variables of both good and bad transference. We are perceived by many as being kind, concerned, comforting and wise. But occasionally we encounter clients who see in us a fierce opponent, or they expect us to be all-knowing masters and perfectly psychic gurus. Or we unconsciously remind them of a parent or authority figure who they are angry with; they then shift their displaced anger onto us. In another situation in a professional practice, we may encounter erotic transference, where clients perceive us as being an ideal potential lover.

In understanding that transference is occurring, we can address the situation directly. We educate the client by identifying the dynamics. By bringing to the surface what is happening unconsciously and then enquiring into the formative influences which are inappropriately playing out in the present, the person achieves greater self-understanding.

Countertransference, where we therapists and readers transfer our emotional reactions onto clients, is just as common and occurs even after years of professional counseling and coaching of others. We experience conscious or unconscious emotional entanglements, such as irritation, or judgment, or getting lost in un-boundaried empathy that is often triggered by their transference, or because they remind us of someone we know.

As readers it is important to avoid adverse effects of our countertransference by being vigilantly aware of our subjective responses. Potentially, both transference and countertransference gift us with insight; there are benefits to unpacking and reflecting on the emotional reactions that arise.

Also worth mentioning is projection, a psychological process that is somewhat similar to transference but relates more specifically to a person attributing their own thoughts, behavioral traits and impulses to another, as if they know what the person is doing or feeling better than they know themselves. They reject their own unacceptable motive, attitude, characteristic or behavior and then accuse the other person of behaving or feeling that same way. The person uses projection as a defense mechanism, as if the best form of defense is attack. Havoc and misunderstandings resulting from projection also occur with 'complimentary' projection, for example, when a client projects onto the reader their assumption that the reader is an all knowing oracle of perfect wisdom. This helps them to feel as if they are in safe hands, but is a distortion of reality. In a chirology practice, the issue of projection is a counseling and coaching theme in itself, that might, for example, arise when clients discuss their partner's behaviors.

Honesty

People come as truth seekers, they want the hard truth, good or bad. The truth, conveyed with virtues of kindness and compassion, is a necessary part of our skill-set. Honesty is the best policy, but here we have a grey zone. Can lies by omission be pardoned, are there occasions when withholding the truth from a client is the right thing to do?

There is a fine line between our need to encourage clients, and their need for authentic honesty. Since white lies are lies that are not intended to harm and indeed are often intended to benefit the person by making them feel good, or preventing their feelings from being hurt, it may feel for the reader that lying is easier than honesty, and that bypassing radical honesty has the magical power to spare pain and preserve comfort. As readers, an alluring option is to "be kind" and to reassure them of happy endings.

While as readers we cannot be absolutely certain of any inevitability in the client's life, there often comes the sense of the likelihood of their desired outcome being bleak. Based on what we see in their hands, what we feel in their energy field, and what we hear in the conversation, we might feel a sense of dread and despair, with an inner knowing of their facing severe restrictions ahead. In these situations, it is not fair for us to engender unrealistic expectations and give hope where there is none.

Clouding the truth might damage our credibility. A courageous enquiry into possible unfavorable outcomes is what is needed most. Far better to let them down as gently as possible. Using the word "warning" is distressing, but by working tactfully, in the context of "in the event of this situation not having the outcome you hope for, how might you support yourself?" we better encourage and empower them. Conversation is directed towards a plan B. Enquiry zones in on defining resources for how they will cope in the event of disappointment.

This being said, there are certain circumstances where information that is un-useful, hurtful and psychologically harmful can be withheld. For example, a client with a rampant cancer asks if they will survive their illness. Our intuitive knowing is perfectly clear, but for this client, who is not yet ready to accept their diagnosis, there might be an intent and purpose to our lying; by withholding our truth we consciously choose to not take away their hope. Evasion of the truth that protects or eases burdens is, under certain circumstances, acceptable. A definitive no, you will not survive this could have negative consequences. In some cases, benevolent lies may be the kindest and most reasonable course of action.

On the other hand, with a different type of client, who is in the same terminal illness situation but who is past the stage of denial, our telling them the truth sets them free and opens the conversation to a deeper intimacy; without our honesty the person would intuitively feel abandoned and disappointed.

Another perspective maintains that radical honesty, regardless of whether it produces good or bad consequences is always best, that in the quantum field no matter what transpires, the client needs to hear, to have that experience, and that they as the querant are 50% responsible, by virtue of their outreach, for what they are told.

A complicated dynamic easily arises when working with couples. By way of one example, a wife, who is first for a reading, reveals that she is having an affair and that she is planning a divorce strategy. In her husband's reading a few days later, he mentions his suspicions, asks "What did she tell you?" and "Can you see in my hands if she is with another man?" In these type of instances, we protect client confidentiality and withhold the truth. Here we have good reason to be as ambiguous as possible, a lie here is self-protective in that it maintains professional boundaries. Even though he is sure at some stage to discover that I, as their reader, in fact knew of her love affair, my maintaining ethical integrity takes precedence over betraying her confidence.

Imposter Syndrome

As a professional chirologist, there are times when self-doubt arises, along with acute "imposter syndrome" attacks. The inner critic assaults with plaguing thoughts and uncertainties, such as "I am not qualified or competent enough" and "Did I say the right thing, did I say the wrong thing, I'm so bad at this" or "I'm a fraud, charlatan, a fake, who do I think I am?" Instead of positively acknowledging ourselves, perfectionism sabotages and we agonize over perceived errors.

Self-doubt is an arch enemy, but paradoxically, self-doubt is also an ally. The inner critic that questions our integrity and competence and propels us to seek professional supervision inhibits any unrealistic sense of our own capabilities. The inner critic is there for a beautiful reason; self-doubt is like an inner coach who shines a clarifying light of internal self-awareness to ensure that we are alert to the shadow parts of ourselves that we aren't usually aware of, don't want to own and might do well to explore. The reflective practice of subjective self-assessment of the standard of our work is by default innately healthy and natural to our work as dialogue therapists.

Burnout

At some point in a long-term hand reading career, the entrée of a deep felt sense of fatigue, of being totally drained and all dried up, is a highly likely, if not inevitable visitor. Worn down from both the years of listening to other people's troubles and the chronic stressors of our personal lives, we find that thoughts and feelings of resistance, of being cynically jaded, of not ever wanting to look at another set of hands and of dreading seeing another client, start creeping in.

In my career as a counseling and coaching chirologist, I've suffered a period of burnout, where I felt utter exhaustion and grave doubt of my professional ability. The imposter syndrome replaced my confidence, I felt like a charlatan and all joy in my work seemed irretrievably lost.

Then I came across this beautifully profound and wise quote (author unfortunately unknown). The words helped me to navigate though and to understand the why of our dark nights of soul exhaustion. In reading and aligning with this wisdom, I now know that burnout was a necessary part of my growth.

"Probably just about everybody who sustains their passion and purpose for the long haul has to undergo some sort of profound transition. Early in our lives, we have enthusiasm, perhaps we are on a quest, ready to take on our life mission, but then over time come the dark nights, of burnout, disillusionment, disinterest. These phases are almost inevitable. Through each of these periods in careers there comes transition as you evolve from enthusiastic and driven mission, to settling into, embracing and fully practicing a chosen vocation. In each transition is passion, and gratitude, and a deep acceptance of your unique knowledge and skill, to re-engage more maturely. The transition of mission to vocation links inextricably with a wiser, steadier, more sustainable kind of passion."

The Reading

A spoken statement before the client arrives that is used to center, ground and protect sets the intention for working for the highest good of all. Personal favorites are the decree "Divine Light of the Highest Order, under the protection of the Archangel St Michael" and the affirmation "I Am guided, protected, directed."

- Alert your client to their nearby glass of water and box of tissues.

- Start with a few moments of silence; breathing together in sacred pause is a highly beneficial way to set the tone for an authentic experience for the person.

- Take your time. Hold and stroke their hands for as long as feels comfortable. Did the person offer their hands facing downwards or upwards? Downwards shows reticence and vulnerability, that it will take time for them to feel safe. Share this with them: "That you have placed your hands facing downwards reveals you to be a private person. It will take me time to gain your trust." The opposite applies with those who reach across and push their hands close to you. Here we have a wonderful enthusiasm but perhaps a deficit of healthy boundaries; this theme might be discussed a little further into the session.

- Be sure to open the conversation with generalized, neutral observations about character, temperament and traits; keep it simple. The first sentences that readers speak have significant impact on the quality of potential rapport and on the overall success of the reading. Don't rush into the deep end. If you go too deep too fast with an out of context or even inaccurate observation, rapport will be impaired; this error

213

would set a disappointed undertone that could irreparably hamper the quality of the entire reading.

- Begin the reading with themes related to the area of life that through observation of the hands is intuitively sensed as being most alive in the person.

- Dialogue in a flexible, fluid way about what comes up for that person, and keep coming around to the most critical of their issues.

- You need not say more than you are personally capable of picking up or intuiting or interpreting. If you run out of things to say, drop into that moment of authentic emptiness. Feeling pressurized results in repetition, overemphasis or even in becoming untrue with what you say. Take a pause, in stillness. Wait. Allowing for pause brings peace; we communicate without speaking. Honor the innate communicative power of the reading experience, forgive yourself, and keep your impeccability. Rather give the reading more non-verbal communicative power.

- Pause periodically and enquire as to how they are feeling now, how is the experience for them so far, this gives clients time and space to feel for and to share what for them is important.

- During the conversation, use their name.

- A note on accuracy: There are times when as reader I recommend a course of action or outline a likely outcome, but my suggestion catalyzes the client's choosing the exact opposite of what's been recommended or anticipated. I am inaccurate and incorrect, yet the conversation is valuable; the enquiry into the one possibility cements its opposite; decisions and changes are then more proactively acted upon.

214

- Choose your vocabulary with care. Use permissive words: maybe, perhaps, could be, possibly, could it be, have you found. Do not use words like but, you need to, you must, you should.

- It is an imperative that we cross-reference the forms and markings of people's hands before reaching conclusions. It cannot be emphasized enough that we ought not to read any one hand feature in isolation.

- For follow-up and future readings, be sure to refer back to their prints in advance, so as to remember who the client is and to refresh your memory of their story.

Ending the Reading

Before bringing the reading to a close, readers are advised to ask the question "How has the experience of this reading been for you?" This question supports the client in that it offers them the opportunity to share any final thoughts or feedback. The asking of this open question also helps us as readers; self-doubt and inner criticism is subdued by the sustaining of our full presence.

A recommended suggestion for hand readers: at the very end of the reading, gently hold together the client's two hands in yours, invite them to close their eyes, and sit for a few moments of sacred pause. A prayerful mention of gratitude to them, yourself, the ancestors, departed loved ones, guides, the angels and God can feel very meaningful for some; do this when it feels right and appropriate.

Ensure that your client is clear about any referrals and recommendations you've offered. Since everything cannot be resolved in one consultation, be sure to emphasize your availability for ongoing support. Invite them to return for follow-up readings so as to focus on the specific issues that have been identified.

Before they leave, shake hands again, or hug them. After they leave, make a few key reference notes about their story and the names of the people in their life; this ensures that you'll remember them when they schedule their next appointment.

- People perceive a reading as a once off thing, but chirology is a short-term intervention coaching and counseling therapy that, when indicated, comprises between 4 - 6 initial consultations, with yearly follow-ups.
- Quality referrals are supportive and are integral to a counseling and coaching chirologist's professionalism. Develop a sound referral list of other specialist practitioners. Clients often ask for, or due to situations that are out of the scope of a chirology practice, need referrals.

Your Professional Practice

Audio Recording

Some readers take the view that a reading is an 'in the now' experience, and that what the client needs, they will take away. They prefer to not record. In another situation, a client might specifically ask that their reading is not recorded. But mostly, our clients realize that remembering everything we discuss is an impossible task; for them, a recording is a helpful and supportive aid.

The practical question of whether or not to record is an air-governed component of the craft; we use technology. Zoom offers an auto record option. In personal readings use a phone or recording device. Mail the .mp3 to the client via any online portal that delivers large files.

Branding and Marketing

Activating a marketing strategy is often the most challenging hurdle for readers, especially if they are unfamiliar with or resistant to technology. Having a website adds credibility and is probably non-negotiable. Your website creates a first impression and informs and clarifies what exactly it is that you offer. Developing a mailing list and sending periodic newsletters with links to your blog articles is recommended for growing your 'tribe'.

Branding is potentially an excitingly creative component of building a professional practice. Your logo, choice of color and fonts symbolically signify what you offer. Do you market under your personal name i.e. yourself as the product, or with another attractive trademark name?

Client Information Questionnaire and Indemnity

Here's an example of a brief questionnaire and indemnity for new clients to fill and sign.

Indemnity

Date_____

Name: _____

Contact Number: _____

email: _____

Date of Birth:_____

I   ._____
take responsibility for any and all consequences for the guidelines and suggestions presented during this consultation. The information and opinions provided are believed to be accurate and sound, based on the best judgment available. No warranty or guarantee is expressed or implied. (Your name) rescinds liability for errors or omissions during the consultation and makes no claims to being a legal, financial or marriage counsellor or medical practitioner. While (your name) will endeavor to assure that the recording device functions, (your name) is not responsible for any malfunction of the recording and subsequent loss of information.

Please signify your assent to this disclaimer.

Signed: _____

Email Bookings

For email bookings, it is helpful to draft a professional appointment confirmation reply template (with all relevant info) for repeat use.

Environment and Seating

Two comfortable wingback chairs with a small table between is my most recommended choice of seating. A pleasant and welcoming environment makes a big difference to your professionalism; beautify your consultation space with flowers, candles, your books and any other ornaments that add to the ambiance. Have water and tissues well-positioned beforehand.

Zoom and Skype Readings

Paradoxically, while touching, holding and stroking people's hands is integral to the craft, online readings based on photographs prove to be very successful. An email template with the specifications for required photographs might look like:

Photographs: (format - .jpg)

- One each of front of each hand, hand held flat against plain background, fingers included
- One each of back of each hand – hand held flat, fingers included
- One each of close ups of palms (to see the lines) - hands held flat
- One each close-up of each thumb tip (for the fingerprint)
- One each close-up of just your four fingertips of each hand – (hold all 4 fingers together - close up pics to see the fingerprints)
- Information:
- Your full name
- Where you are in the world (for time differences)
- Are you are right or left handed?
- Your date of birth

Index

Other publications by Jennifer:

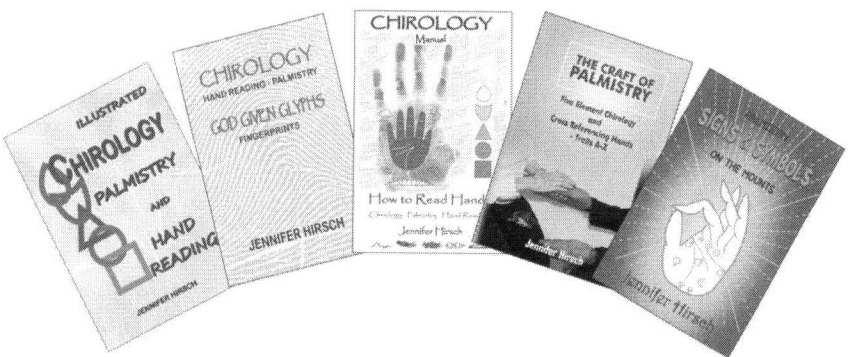

Illustrated Chirology Palmistry and Hand Reading

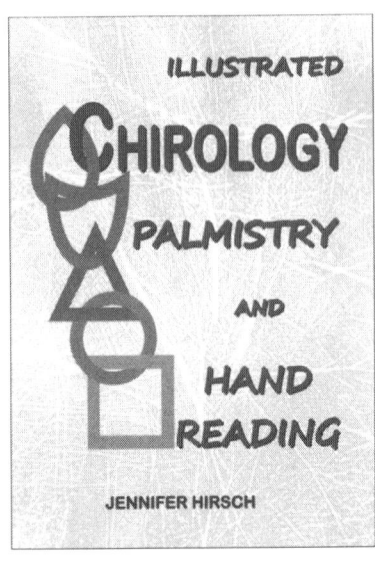

The essential guide for hand readers. Designed for hand reading beginners and experts alike, this chirology and palmistry reference guidebook is an encyclopedic presentation of hundreds of tutorials, illustrations, photographs and hand print samples. The informative and easy to read lessons offer a step-by-step systematic approach to the study and practice of chirology and palmistry.

Illustrated Chirology Palmistry and Hand Reading includes:

- All the information needed to become a confident and proficient hand reader.
- Explorations of all aspects of past and present trends of the craft of hand reading.
- References to scientific health research and hands.
- In-depth explanations of the element system of interpretation.
- Tried and tested meanings handed down from traditional western palmistry systems.
- Know-how for using chirology and palmistry as a diagnostic tool to genuinely understand yourself and others.
- Information about the significance and role of intuitive perception and psychic attunement in the hand reading craft.
- Suggestions and techniques for how to trust yourself and

your integrity as a hand reader.

- Guidelines on how-to listen and how to speak; your verbal delivery, structured within the 5 Realms counseling and coaching model.
- Hundreds of illustrations to help you to identify and interpret the shapes, textures, dermatoglyphics, lines and all other features of the hands.
- A clear and thorough investigation into each and every component of the hand readers craft.

https://www.amazon.com/Jennifer-Hirsch/e/B07QC3JL2H/ref=ntt_dp_epwbk_0
https://www.smashwords.com/books/view/934811

Chirology - Hand Reading - Palmistry
God Given Glyphs - Fingerprints

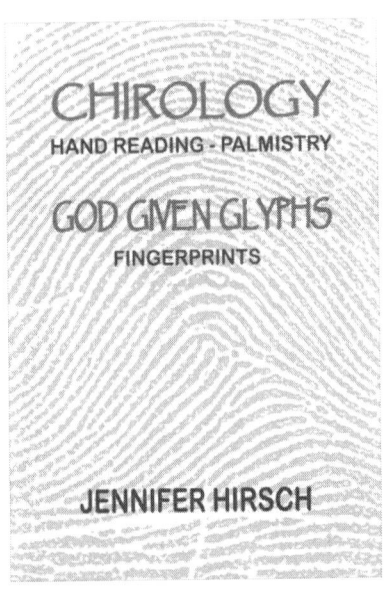

A comprehensive chirology 'bible', designed to draw attention to the newest developments in hand reading today. First published in 2009, the book presents a fresh look at the significance of glyph skin ridge patterns in the powerful counseling and coaching modality that is chirology. Our fingerprints, the dermatoglyphic symbols that are inscribed upon our hands, are not only an irrefutable mark of our identity - they also describe individual psychological profiles, each with their own unique signature traits. This definitive glyph pattern guidebook enables you to easily identify your individual fingerprint patterns, so as to understand more about yourself; physically, emotionally, vocationally, mentally and spiritually. Guaranteed to capture your imagination, the illustrations are accompanied by meanings for when the glyph patterns are on thumbs, index, middle, ring and baby fingers, and the palm. Jennifer Hirsch presents over 200 images of the cosmic patterns that cover our palmar surfaces. The samples were chosen from her collection and include contributions from police records.

https://www.amazon.com/Jennifer-Hirsch/e/B07QC3JL2H/ref=ntt_dp_epwbk_0

Chirology Manual - How to Read Hands:
Chirology - Palmistry - Hand Reading

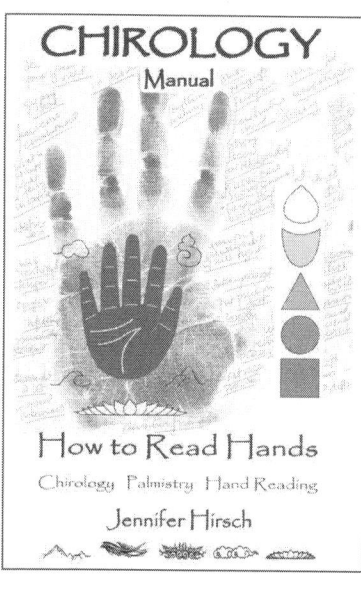

Jennifer Hirsch presents her extensively illustrated, systematically presented and easy to understand training manual. Developed over many years of teaching chirology to hundreds of students both in and out of South Africa.

This book includes:

- Guide to how to take hand prints.
- An in-depth explanation of the five element system of how to interpret hands.
- The Five Realm model of counseling and coaching with chirology.
- Discussions about prediction and intuition.
- Meanings for handshakes, gestures, sizes and colors of hands.
- Explanations of the relevance of hand shapes and skin textures.
- Presentations on all the palmar mounts.
- Digital dermatoglyphics and their meanings.
- Illustrated section and meanings of palmar dermatoglyphics.
- Extensive coverage of all possible finger and thumb formations.

- All the know-how you'll need about palmar lines.
- Visual representations of many palmar markings and their tried and tested accurate meanings.
- 208 of illustrations.
- A comprehensive reference index.
- and so much more ....

https://www.amazon.com/Jennifer-Hirsch/e/B07QC3JL2H/ref=ntt_dp_epwbk_0
https://www.smashwords.com/books/view/934614

The Craft of Palmistry:

Five Element Chirology and
Cross Referencing Hands - Traits A - Z

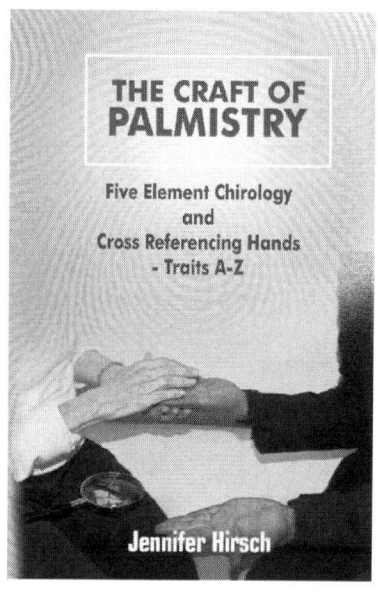

A book comprising two parts. Section one is a simple, yet comprehensive and very beautifully illustrated guide that will teach you to read own and other's hands.

Emphasis is on the Five Element system of interpretation.

The second part of this book contains 26 illustrations of different traits which are designed to help you to cross reference hands for markings that back up and verify the accuracy of your interpretation of people's hands.

Chirology is a counseling tool, a dialogue therapy and a healing modality.

The blending of ancient five element Chinese Buddhist hand reading principles with the lore of traditional western palmistry enables you to accurately identify the markings on hands that depict skills and character traits.

Find out how to identify signs of ambition, creativity, honesty, jealousy, psychic ability etc.

Over 200 human traits are illustrated, within 26 alphabetical themes. An extensive glossary explains each marking in greater depth.

https://www.amazon.com/Jennifer-Hirsch/e/B07QC3JL2H/ref=ntt_dp_epwbk_0

Palmistry - Signs & Symbols on the Mounts

What might a cross, pentagram, square, star, triangle or other symbol signify? Old palmistry tradition holds that each symbol reveals either gain or loss, luck or trouble, peace or conflict, honesty or deceit, along with many other possibilities. The energies that the symbol exudes activates the intuitive palm reader's psychic perceptions. By getting our brains out the way, and instead allowing soul self to guide us, we tap into the mystical skills of the chiromancers of the past.

The special signs and symbols are sometimes hard to identify. Suited for beginner and advanced palm readers, the how-to of both finding and interpreting the markings is presented in this vividly illustrated book.

"Palmistry Signs & Symbols on the Mounts" includes:
• Over 100 hand prints with stunning close-up images of the symbols.
• Explanations of the historical symbology of the palmar mounts.
• Each mount's associated qualities and characteristics
• Well researched traditional and up to date meanings for the special signs and symbols on the mounts.
• Preservation of the amusing fatalistic meanings of yesteryear.
• A look into Gypsy palm reading and fortune telling.
• Information about the link between palmistry and astrology.

The special signs and symbols in hands have only ever been illustrated in drawings. In this treasure of a book, I have presented examples directly from over 80 actual palm prints.

https://www.amazon.com/Jennifer-Hirsch/e/B07QC3JL2H/ref=ntt_dp_epwbk_0

Printed in Great Britain
by Amazon

68066993R00138